THE FRANCHISEE
Playbook
2ND EDITION

A STEP-BY-STEP MANUAL FOR CHOOSING A WINNING FRANCHISE

RICK BISIO and **BRITT SCHROETER**

Disclaimer

This workbook is designed to provide accurate guidance in regard to the subject matter covered. You purchase this workbook with the understanding that neither the authors nor the publisher is engaged in rendering legal, investment, or accounting services. If these services are required, the appropriate expertise should be secured.

All examples and tables in this workbook are for illustration only and do not represent any specific franchise or individual.

© 2020 Second Edition The Franchisee Playbook
By Rick Bisio and Britt Schroeter
Cover Design by PytchBlack
ISBN-10: 170-910-40-31
ISBN-13: 978-1-709104-03-9

© 2011 First Edition
By Rick Bisio and Britt Schroeter
Cover and interior design by Harry Beckwith for Hot Pixel Group
ISBN-10: 1-935098-54-3
ISBN-13: 978-1-935098-54-6
Bascom Hill Publishing Group
https://bascomhillpublishing.com

Printed in the United States of America.

Other Books by Rick Bisio

The Educated Franchisee: Find the Perfect Franchise for You, Third Edition; The Insider's Guide (Tasora Books, 2017)

Note: This workbook frequently references *The Educated Franchisee*. If you have not read this best-selling book on franchising, please do so. Certain content is baseline knowledge, better suited for the book than the workbook. You can purchase a copy wherever fine books are sold.

Anne-Lise, Ella, and Luke:
To begin the day with your smile and end the day with your kiss.
Simply the definition of the perfect day.
Thank You.
~ R. Bisio

For my three best friends:
Caron, Jack, and Bill.
You are my inspiration. You are my joy.
You are my forever sunshine.
~ B. Schroeter

Table of Contents

List of Exercises

Acknowledgments

FROM RICK BISIO

After writing *The Educated Franchisee* there were a number of people who suggested a companion workbook. Easy to say, but hard to do.

How do you take the due-diligence process and break it down into manageable steps—steps that will work no matter the franchise and no matter the prospective franchisee? I did not know the answer, but I knew that Britt Schroeter was the right partner for this project. The only way this workbook would happen would be with her as my co-author.

Not only does Britt have the ability to break things apart into bit-size chunks, she also has the patience and thoughtfulness of a wonderful teacher. I am truly fortunate that Britt agreed to this odyssey. Britt, I cannot thank you enough.

FROM BRITT SCHROETER

Rick, it's been an honor working as your co-author. I never imagined the commitment required to complete this workbook, though you warned me. Without you by my side, I would have put down the pen a thousand times. But you always inspired me to pick it back up. Writing a book collaboratively has been an adventure. I can't think of anyone else with whom I could have completed this venture. Like raising a child, this has taken teamwork, patience, and true collaboration. You have made this an amazing learning experience and an amazing time, with a spectacular finished product. I am proud to have you as a friend, business associate, and now as a co-author.

FROM BOTH AUTHORS

We would both like to thank the many people that reviewed the workbook in its early stages, providing invaluable feedback: Jennifer Gehlhar, Deb Percival, Scott Jones, Kim Daly, Melissa Lewis, and Mike Kohler. Each one of your thoughtful comments improved this workbook and helped make it what it is today.

Life is a process of learning. To everyone that has taken the time to help us learn, those that have taught us in the classrooms, those that have taught us in our careers, and those that have taught us about life, your teachings are reflected in these pages. For you, our teachers, we are forever grateful.

Preface

The United States is an amazing story of entrepreneurship. The United States was not "founded," it was "boot-strapped." And it was not built by the wealthy elite; it was built by brave and hardworking immigrants who believed in a better future. These immigrants started businesses, raised families, and built a country. This pioneering spirit is still alive. It is part of us—all of us. From the Kansas housewife to the Harvard MBA, this workbook can help you call out your pioneering spirit.

Today more and more people look to escape the insecurity of corporate America. But how do you do this? How do you take control—safely? Here is the reality: franchising is the most transparent business format ever created! You can literally learn everything you need to know about a franchise opportunity before you invest a penny.

You don't have to be a genius. These secrets are not just for those "in the know." Anyone can do it. All you have to do is follow the steps outlined in this workbook.

Franchise due diligence is all about knowing what questions to ask. You must know what you want and be fully focused on finding it. You need to be organized and directed in your search. You need the best information and you need to know how to verify the information.

Can you do this on your own, without the support of this workbook?

Of course you can, but it is likely you will miss critical investigation steps. *The Franchisee Playbook* is designed to make sure you don't miss a thing. Don't misunderstand—this will be work. Analyzing franchise opportunities will demand time and energy. It will test your commitment.
But think about this. If you are not willing to put the time into the due diligence, how successful will you be as a business owner?

This workbook, quite frankly, is your first test.

The Franchisee Playbook is designed to help you get organized. Get focused. Drive the process. If you follow the simple, step-by-step instructions, you will find yourself gaining knowledge and insight. You will find yourself doing. Eventually, you will find yourself educated.

Although the process is important, *The Franchisee Playbook* is all about the end result. When you focus your energy on the process you will find yourself moving toward the best end result for you. Each person will gain different insight from this process but the answers that emerge will allow you to gain confidence in regard to business and franchise ownership.

The system we share in *The Franchisee Playbook* has been extraordinarily successful! And if a franchise is all about systems, doesn't it make perfect sense to tap a proven system to make the best decision? Your willingness to follow the steps in this workbook alone begins to shed light on your appropriateness for franchising.

The Franchisee Playbook teaches you how to gather the facts and how to make smart decisions. Buying a business is more than just the facts. It takes emotional commitment. This workbook addresses your most intuitive, emotional side, but not until your foundation is in place, a foundation based on due diligence, logic, and facts. No decisions are made until the homework is done.

So, what results can you expect?

About one third of the people who complete this workbook will conclude that business ownership is not for them, period. And for that group that will be the right outcome. Business ownership is not for everyone. This workbook is designed to flush out the folks that should simply remain employees from the folks that should become entrepreneurs. The world needs both to go around.

Another third of readers who are diligent in completion of this workbook will become business owners, with strong, proven franchise systems. For that group, we want to be the first to say, Congratulations!

For the final third, the news is not so great. This last third will continue to dream of entrepreneurship. They will speak to their friends about what they are going to do—one day. But they will never do it. For those folks, our hope is that this workbook will deliver clarity. We want you to be able to confidently determine whether business ownership is right for you—Yes or No.

Not a "maybe . . ."

Not an "I wish . . ."

Not an "I want to but . . ."

The Franchisee Playbook pushes you through indecision. It requires courage . . . and work. But found within these pages you will discover the tools to make a confident, educated decision.

Welcome to the road of discovery. Good travels and good luck.

Step 1: Define Your Vision—Your Magic Wand

"The future belongs to those who believe in the beauty of their dreams."

~ Eleanor Roosevelt (1884-1962)
First Lady of the United States and civil rights advocate

PURPOSE

» **Think about what makes you happy and proud.**

» **Clearly define a vision for yourself.**

» **Make your vision come to life!**

If presented with two gifts, but you could only choose one—crystal ball or a magic wand—which would you choose? Would you rather be able to see your future or control your future? Most of us would choose the ability to control the future.

As Lewis Carroll so aptly stated, "If you don't know where you are going, any road will get you there." The purpose of this first set of exercises is to define your destination. Only then can you set the course. A succinct vision statement will provide both direction and motivation as you move toward a better future with clarity and purpose.

Over the years we have worked with scores of men and women who dream of business ownership. What do the men and women who have made this dream a reality share that others do not? It all begins with vision. Successful entrepreneurs know where they want to go. Having a clear, focused vision generates the strength and tenacity to take control and make things happen.

Your current vision may be "to become a business owner." This first set of exercises is designed to show you how to create a more powerful vision, including how to incorporate measurement standards that will lead you into a more vibrant future of your own design.

WHERE ARE YOU TODAY?

Before you create your own vision statement, you must take stock of where you are today. It is important to be able to identify what makes you happy now and express a sense of gratitude for what you already have.

✎ EXERCISE 1.1: WHAT MAKES ME HAPPY?

In this exercise, list the things that bring you happiness. What are you most excited to tell your family and friends about? What creates the spark?

1. _____
2. _____
3. _____
4. _____
5. _____
6. _____
7. _____
8. _____

✎ EXERCISE 1.2: WHAT MAKES ME PROUD?

Now, think about and list the things you are most proud of.

1. _____
2. _____
3. _____
4. _____
5. _____
6. _____
7. _____
8. _____

EXERCISE 1.3: THE MOST IMPORTANT THINGS IN MY LIFE

Now write down the 10 most important things in your life. Once you have completed this list, rank these items from most important (#1) to least important (#10).

Rank

1. _____ _____

2. _____ _____

3. _____ _____

4. _____ _____

5. _____ _____

6. _____ _____

7. _____ _____

8. _____ _____

9. _____ _____

10. _____ _____

NOTES

_____

_____

_____

_____

_____

_____

_____

LOOK TOWARD THE FUTURE

Now that you have examined where you are in life by identifying the things that make you happy and proud, and thought about what is most important to you, it's time to build your vision for the future.

The best place to start is at the end. How will you know you focused on what was most important? How will you know you have left the world a little better because you were here?

Imagine that you are seventy-five years old and have led a noteworthy life. As a result, you have been invited back to your high school to be the keynote speaker at graduation. Imagine the introduction. What do you want to hear the principal say about you? As you write this, pay close attention to what would be said now (given your existing credentials) versus what you would like to be said in the future.

✏ EXERCISE 1.4: MY FUTURE INTRODUCTION

Now, write your desired introduction for your future here:

Please join me in welcoming . . . _____

_____

_____

_____

_____

_____

_____

_____

_____

_____

_____

_____

_____

EXERCISE 1.5: MY LIFE INSIGHTS

Next, what would you tell your audience? What are the key points that you would want them to remember? How can they lead a significant life free of regrets?

During my life I learned . . . _____

_____

_____

_____

_____

_____

_____

_____

_____

_____

_____

_____

_____

_____

_____

_____

_____

_____

_____

_____

_____

_____

_____

CREATE YOUR VISION STATEMENT

You are almost there. Now you have everything you need to create a succinct personal vision statement. Your vision statement should not include the words "business" or "job." Statements such as "I want to be a business owner" or "I want to be an employee" are not powerful personal visions. Use your thoughts from the earlier exercises. Work them into your vision. A vision statement should capture that which brings you happiness and should clarify that which is most important to you. A clear personal vision is the cornerstone to a life plan and the only way to know if you are moving in the right direction.

Ideally, your vision statement will be less than 125 words. It should be written in present tense and you should use words that you find emotionally powerful. Your vision statement should contain specific, measurable outcomes and a target date for accomplishing those outcomes. The measurable outcome and target date should include financial goals. What will it cost you to retire? What will it cost you to achieve the vision you have created? When do you hope to retire? Some people aim for a total net worth by a certain age—for example, "I want to have $1 million in the bank by age sixty-five." Other people aim to maintain their income level: "I want to continue to earn $80,000 a year until the end of my life." Still others set a monthly net passive income goal (net passive income is the total amount of income you receive from your investments after paying taxes): "I want to earn $5,000 per month in net passive or semi-passive income." All of these strategies can work, but for the purpose of this workbook you must establish an annual cost for retirement. The annual cost of your vision is determined by the goals you set forth now.

In step 4 we will re-examine your annual cost and you may find yourself adjusting this number up or down after closer examination. But we want you to have a starting point, a current goal to work from. The point is: if you don't know what retirement will cost each year, you will not be able to determine if financially you will be able to retire.

Your vision will serve as a tool. It needs to capture the spirit of where you want to go and who you want to be. Don't worry about how you will get there . . . yet. Remember, the vision is your destination and the job or business is the vehicle.

If you need help writing your vision statement, here are several simple yet powerful vision statements that may inspire you.

CASE STUDY: CARON AND JACK'S VISION

What is most important to us is our family. We are living a life that allows continuous focus on our priorities. We "work to live" not "live to work." We control our future. We set our own work hours and set our own play hours. By age fifty-five we will have passive or semi-passive income streams producing a minimum of $80,000 a year. This allows us to spend the majority of our time doing the things we love: being with family, traveling, skiing, fishing, and celebrating life. We will own a home in the Florida Keys.

CASE STUDY: ELLA AND LUKE'S VISION

Our vision is centered on family and flexibility. We have young children and want to be a part of their lives as they grow. We want to be available for them every day, while also giving them the things they need to become strong, well-balanced adults. We will retire at age fifty-eight. By this point, we will have developed a passive (or semi-passive) income of $5,000 per month after our fixed expenses. This disposable income will give us the freedom and flexibility to travel and explore other countries at our own pace well into our retirement years.

CASE STUDY: JOHN AND TONYA'S VISION

We are a God-loving family and feel that our purpose here on earth is to share the good work of the Lord. We look toward retirement and missionary work as an exciting transition in our lives. To do this effectively, we need to save a minimum of $1 million and invest this at 8%, producing $80K per year. Ideally, we would save considerably more than this during our working years. Missionary work is not expensive, but the more money we have the more we can give and the more good we can do for others.

EXERCISE 1.6: MY VISION FOR THE FUTURE

Write your vision here:

_____

_____

_____

_____

_____

_____

_____

_____

_____

_____

_____

_____

_____

_____

✎ EXERCISE 1.7: COST OF MY VISION

Re-read your vision above. What is the annual cost to achieve your vision? Rewrite the cost of your vision below. We will return to this number throughout the workbook. This cost may adjust as you gain more knowledge, but identify your initial goal here:

Annual cost of my vision: _____

EXPLORE YOUR VISION

It is time to explore your vision. Make it more detailed, more alive. It is your vision and you need to own it. Here are some ideas—be sure to complete at least one of these exercises.

✎ EXERCISE 1.8: DEDICATING TO MY VISION

☐ Are you a visual person? If so, you should draw or paint your vision.

☐ Not an artist? Make a dream board. Cut out pictures from magazines that represent your vision and then tape or glue them to a poster board. Its okay to post the picture of the twin red Lamborghini's, but don't forget to capture all that is important to you, not just the material things.

☐ Not a visual person? If you like to write, take some time to write a story about your vision, and the life you will be leading. Make sure the words speak to your heart!

☐ Are you an auditory person? Make a recording of your vision and put it on your iPod.

☐ As a final step, make sure you can see or hear your vision every day. Make it your screensaver, post it throughout your home and office, or carry it around in your wallet.

"**I understand** . . . all great adventures, all noble pursuits, and all life-changing actions begin in the mind. It is not possible to know the right course of action unless I have a vision for my future. I have a clear vision for where I want my life to take me and the vision is firmly grounded in my mind and in my heart."

X _____   X _____

       Signature   **Date**

Step 2: Identify and Leverage Common Fears

"Courage is resistance to fear, mastery of fear—not absence of fear."

~ Mark Twain (1835–1910)
American author and humorist

PURPOSE

» **Identify your past and current fears.**

» **Identify proven strategies you have used to overcome your fears.**

» **Identify your fears surrounding entrepreneurship.**

» **Fully commit to due diligence focused on knowledge acquisition.**

Fear! Why do we have a set of exercises on fear? There are two simple reasons:

The first is because fear is the one thing that can, and too often does, stop us dead in our tracks. Fear is a monster that takes root in our minds. It starts under the bed as a child, then it moves into the closet, and it eventually walks with all of us as we grow and mature. Fear can rob us of the ability to achieve our dreams.

The second reason is to help you learn how to harness fear and use it to your advantage. Successful entrepreneurs learn how to identify their fear and use it to propel them toward success. Motivational studies tell us there are two primary motivators in life. One is *the desire to succeed*. The other is the *desire to avoid failure*. These studies also tell us that the desire to avoid failure is tremendously powerful. In fact, for many, the desire to avoid failure is a primary motivational factor in success. Successful people hate failing, so they work harder, prepare better, and, in the end, they succeed more.

It is not uncommon for us to have a prospective franchisee call to say, "We worked together a few years ago, but I got scared—I decided to play it safe and take a job offer. Here I am, again—laid off again, unhappy again, at the will of an employer again. I sure wish I had moved forward with a business when we first talked. Now I am ready to be a business owner. Can we work together . . . again?"

This process of investigation is going to create anxiety. That is completely normal. But you are going to have to learn how to work through your anxiety to reach your vision.

Have you ever asked a senior citizen if they have anything they regret about their life? If not, try it. Few will talk about what they regret doing. Most often what they will share is what they regret NOT doing.

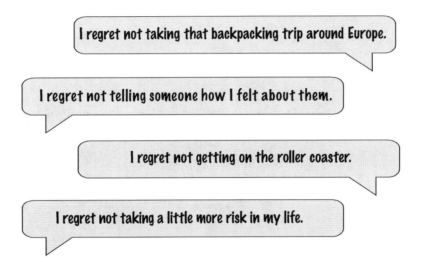

I regret not taking that backpacking trip around Europe.

I regret not telling someone how I felt about them.

I regret not getting on the roller coaster.

I regret not taking a little more risk in my life.

With age comes the wisdom that it is better to try and fail then to never try at all. By coincidence, we both have this same quote on our office walls.

"Life is not a journey to the grave with the intention of arriving safely in a pretty and well-preserved body, but rather to skid in sideways, thoroughly used up, totally worn out, and loudly proclaiming, "WOW, WHAT A RIDE!"

— Author Unknown

The point is to not be afraid. This is the message we want to bring to you. We promise to give you the tools to reduce the risk and make smart, well-informed decisions. You need to promise to emotionally commit to the ride.

IDENTIFY YOUR FEARS

Contemplate the main fears you experienced as a child. Reflect on how you worked through those fears. When you were six years old, what were the things you feared? If you don't remember, call your parents, an older sibling, or someone who knew you at a young age.

✎ EXERCISE 2.1: MY FEARS AS A CHILD

Write your childhood fears here:

1. _____

2. _____

3. _____

4. _____

5. _____

Many of us may have written, "fear of the dark." Think back to when you were young. Why were you afraid of the dark? Did you fear that you could not see the monsters under your bed? Were you afraid of robbers lurking in the shadows? Did you simply relate to the dark as the overwhelming sense of the unknown?

✎ EXERCISE 2.2: MY STRATEGIES TO OVERCOME FEAR AS A CHILD

Are you still afraid of the dark? Are you still afraid of any of your five identified fears? If not, how did you work through or overcome each fear? If any of these fears still exist, how could you work through them?

1. _____

_____

2. _____

_____

3. _____

_____

4. _____

_____

5. _____

_____

To overcome fears, you need to be able to identify them and their root causes. You need to understand how you have worked through fears in the past and plan how to move beyond current fears to achieve growth.

EXERCISE 2.3: MY FEARS AS AN ADULT

As an adult, what fears have you had (or still have)? Be honest—we all have fears.

1. _____

2. _____

3. _____

4. _____

5. _____

6. _____

EXERCISE 2.4: MY STRATEGIES TO OVERCOME FEAR AS AN ADULT

What have you done or could you do to overcome each of these fears?

1. _____

_____

2. _____

_____

3. _____

_____

4. _____

_____

5. _____

_____

6. _____

_____

EXERCISE 2.5: TECHNIQUES TO OVERCOME FEAR

Examine the fears that you have had throughout your life. Which techniques did you use to overcome these fears in order to achieve personal growth? Feel free to write in specific examples after each item.

Acquisition of knowledge: _____

Observation/modeling: _____

Practice: _____

Action: _____

Change in your behavior pattern: _____

Change in your thought process: _____

Change in your environment: _____

Trust in your Creator: _____

Support from friends/family: _____

Trust/belief in your self: _____

EXERCISE 2.6: MY ENTREPRENEURSHIP FEARS

In terms of entrepreneurship, what fears do you have? Brainstorm all of your fears and anxieties as related to entrepreneurship. Some of these fears may begin with questions, such as, "What happens if . . ."

1. _____

_____

2. _____

_____

3. _____

_____

4. _____

_____

5. _____

_____

THE ENTREPRENEUR FEAR BOX

The Entrepreneur Fear Box will help you identify and label your fears about business ownership. Once identified, you will break each fear into specific questions that you can research. Each time you identify a new fear, write it in its own Fear Box. Once it's in a Fear Box, you can focus your energies on gaining information. This process also ensures fear will not overwhelm you, halting progress and knowledge acquisition. Here is an example of a completed Fear Box:

EXAMPLE: ENTREPRENEUR FEAR BOX

Description of Fear: What happens if I go out of business?

Related Questions:

- ✔ How many people have closed their doors with this franchise?
- ✔ What total percentage of the system has gone out of business?
- ✔ Why did they go out of business?

Analysis Steps:

- ✔ Review the Disclosure Document for success and failure rates.
- ✔ Interview the franchise leadership on this issue.
- ✔ Call and interview both current and past franchisees on this issue.
- ✔ Call and interview successful franchisees: What are the traits, skills, and secrets that make them successful?

Knowledge Gained:

- ✔ 88% of franchisees are still in business after three years of operation.
- ✔ The top owners have superior people-management skills, have a strong system orientation, and enjoy multi-tasking.
- ✔ The lowest-performing owners are not committed to advertising budgets, they lack people skills, and they do not follow the systems as they are designed.
- ✔ Owners who left the system were undercapitalized or they had unrealistic expectations in terms of the work level and break-even points.
- ✔ To ensure success, I must understand and be committed to following the systems. I must have proper capitalization and strong people skills.

For additional copies of Fear Boxes go to the download section at: https://educatedfranchisee.com/downloads

---

ENTREPRENEUR FEAR BOX

Description of Fear: _____

Related Questions:

_____

_____

_____

_____

_____

Analysis Steps:

_____

_____

_____

_____

_____

_____

Knowledge Gained:

_____

_____

_____

_____

_____

_____

_____

_____

_____

_____

_____

FEAR AMPLIFIERS

Even if you have completely measured and controlled all aspects of your own fears, there are others around you who may still be fearful. These people are "fear amplifiers." It is just as important to be aware of their feelings as your own.

Do not forget: you are not the only one who this change will affect. If married, your spouse will have to be confident with the decision. How do you turn someone who may be initially skeptical into someone who is supportive? Do not wait till the end of your research to involve your spouse in the decision. It is important to assure your spouse that no decisions will be made independent of his or her feelings, and that everyone needs to be 100% behind any decision made before it is final. For that to happen, your spouse needs to fully participate in the investigations so that together you can make an informed decision based on knowledge, not fear. Also, ask your spouse to work through this workbook with you.

At some point you will decide to share your idea with other individuals besides your spouse, such as friends, co-workers, parents, and siblings. Let us make one thing perfectly clear. Most folks you share this idea with will say something along the lines of:

> "What? A franchise? Are you crazy? My great uncle twice removed on my wife's side had a neighbor in the old neighborhood named Gino. He opened a business importing Italian sausage; and, rumor has it the business did not do well. What makes you think you are better than Gino?"

Unfortunately, though well-intentioned, much of the advice that will come your way will be misguided. Some of the folks you turn to may have little knowledge of business, never mind knowledge of franchising or of a specific industry. Also, those closest to you may be the most conservative in their advice. "Don't change, play it safe. What is wrong with how things are now?"

This process of education will require courage and an ability to stand apart from the crowd. Be prepared! If you know you need support in this area, read the best seller *Feel the Fear and Do It Anyway*, by Susan Jeffers, PhD. This book will help to strengthen your resolve and commitment to proper due diligence, while not allowing others to deflate your dreams.

Fear stunts personal growth. Fear will rob you of control. Instead, let fear motivate you to acquire knowledge and improve your ability to make great decisions. Your success as a business owner depends on it.

"**I promise** . . . I will not allow fear to stop me dead in my tracks. I will identify and work through every fear. I will model successful entrepreneurs and leverage fear to propel me toward success. I will seek knowledge so I am in the position to make an informed and educated decision."

X _____   X _____

Signature   **Date**

Step 3: Review Your Finances

"Whatever the mind of man can conceive and believe, it can achieve. Thoughts are things! And powerful things at that, when mixed with definiteness of purpose, and burning desire, they can be translated into riches."

~ Napoleon Hill (1883–1970)
American author of personal success literature

PURPOSE

» Define your current net worth.

» Define your current household cash flow.

» Determine a maximum investment level.

You have created a vision for your future. You know where you want to go. Now it is time to get a clear picture of where you stand today. These exercises will begin to bring financial clarity to your search. They will help you evaluate your financial position to determine if franchising could be for you. You will determine your net worth and how much you could comfortably afford to invest in a business. These exercises will also help you understand your personal/ family cash flow or current living expenses. This is critical baseline data for future steps. You will use this information as you compile business cash-flow projections and contemplate the financial viability for each franchise you investigate.

NET-WORTH CALCULATION

First you need to calculate your net worth. In simple terms, your net worth is what you own minus what you owe. As you look at franchises, you need to know what you can reasonably afford. To invest more than you can afford is foolish. Most franchisors will not allow someone to invest more than 50% of their net worth in their franchise. Your net worth becomes an initial sorting tool as you begin to focus on potential matches. Websites such as http://www. franchise.org list net-worth requirements for most franchise options.

When completing this next exercise you will notice furniture, boats, jewelry, etc., have not been included in net-worth calculations. Most lenders will NOT be interested in those assets, unless you plan to liquidate them. (If you plan to liquidate any of these assets, calculate their resale value and put that number on the "Other Assets" line.)

✎ EXERCISE 3.1: CURRENT NET WORTH

Use this exercise to determine your current net worth.

CATEGORY	CURRENT VALUE
ASSETS	
Cash in Savings and Checking Accounts	
CDs/Money Market Accounts	
Stocks/Bonds/Mutual Funds	
Other Investments	
Retirement Accounts (e.g., 401(k))	
Market Value of Your Home	
Market Value of Other Real Estate	
Other Assets	
TOTAL ASSETS:	
LIABILITIES	
Mortgages/Home Equity Loans	
Bank Loans	
Student Loans	
Other Loans	
Credit Card Balances	
Other Debts	
TOTAL LIABILITIES:	
NET WORTH (total assets less total liabilities):	

CURRENT HOUSEHOLD CASH FLOW

It is important to understand your household's current monthly income and expenses. You will use this information throughout this workbook.

EXERCISE 3.2: CURRENT MONTHLY INCOME

INCOME CATEGORY	AMOUNT RECEIVED MONTHLY
Your Salary	
Your Spouse's Salary	
Interest and Dividend Income	
Investment and Rental Income	
Business Income	
Alimony/Child Support	
Other Income	
CURRENT MONTHLY INCOME:	

"The life that conquers is the life that moves with a steady resolution and persistence toward a predetermined goal. Those who succeed are those who have thoroughly learned the immense importance of a plan in life, and the tragic brevity of time."

—W.J. Davison

Use the following worksheet to determine your personal living expenses (how much money it costs for you to live for one month). Each person is different so you may not have all these expenses and/or you may have some expenses that are not on this list. Please customize the list to fit your reality.

EXERCISE 3.3: PERSONAL MONTHLY LIVING EXPENSES

EXPENSE CATEGORY	AMOUNT PAID MONTHLY
LOANS	
Home Loan—Mortgage	
Home Loan—Equity Line	
Home Loan—Other Properties	
Car Loan(s)	
Student Loan(s)	
Other Loans	
INSURANCE	
Home	
Car	
Health	
Life	
TAXES	
Home	
Investment and Rental Property	
Other	
UTILITIES	
Electricity	
Water and Sewer	
Natural Gas or Oil	
Communication (Phone, Cell, Internet)	
INVESTMENTS AND SAVINGS	
401(k) or IRA	
Other Investments and Savings	

EXPENSE CATEGORY	AMOUNT PAID MONTHLY
OTHER	
Food	
Child Care	
Alimony/Child Support	
Fuel	
Clothing	
Toiletries, Household Products	
Gifts/Donations	
Grooming (Hair, Make-up, Other)	
Entertainment	
Other	
TOTAL EXPENSES:	

✎ EXERCISE 3.4: MONTHLY NET SAVINGS

In order to determine if you are currently on track to meet your goals, you must subtract your monthly expense from your monthly income.

Current Monthly Income – Personal Monthly Living Expenses = Current Monthly Net Savings
(See page 21)   (See above)

_____ – _____ = _____

Are your personal monthly living expenses higher than you thought? If so, what can you do to reduce them? Achieving your vision usually requires some belt-tightening. This is your chance to measure your current situation and to make adjustments. It is important to understand what your personal expenses will be if you decide to open a business. Will you be able to pay your bills? What type of financing may be required to ensure you have the cash reserves to cover not only the business expenses but also personal living expenses?

MAXIMUM INVESTMENT LEVEL

If you were going to buy a house you would not jump in the car and randomly look at houses. The first step is to get pre-approved for financing so you know what you can afford. Once you know what you can afford, you only look at homes within your price range.

You need to do the same thing before looking at businesses. In order to determine your maximum investment level, you need to evaluate several factors. The first is your current net worth. Most people should not invest more than 50% of their total net worth in a business. This is, in most situations, your maximum investment.

✎ EXERCISE 3.5: MAXIMUM INVESTMENT LEVEL (50% RULE)

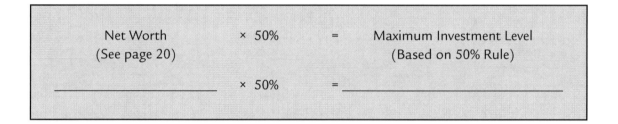

Net Worth (See page 20)	× 50%	=	Maximum Investment Level (Based on 50% Rule)
_____	× 50%	=	_____

However, for many people, the true maximum investment level is lower. Your actual maximum investment level is determined by your assets, liabilities, personal monthly living expenses, credit score, and risk tolerance. Due to the many variations, it is generally not possible to determine this on your own. We suggest you contact funding organizations that specialize in franchise financing. They will be able to give you valuable insights into setting a maximum investment level. (See https://educatedfranchisee.com/resources/franchise-funding-finance)

Most lenders who specialize in franchise financing will be open to an initial discussion to review your specific loan options and to explain the terms of those options. Just because you have set your maximum at a certain dollar amount does not mean that this amount will be all cash out of pocket. Most franchisees finance a portion or all of their investment. In step 12, we will assist you in identifying the ideal loan option. If you feel more comfortable setting your maximum investment amount after completion of that step, please jump to step 12 now. It is never too early to talk with lenders to better understand your specific options. There is power in knowledge. Taking this step now will ensure that you are focused on the appropriate investment level.

✎ EXERCISE 3.6: MAXIMUM FINANCIAL INVESTMENT

Before moving on, think about your risk tolerance. Look in to the resources mentioned earlier and determine your maximum financial investment:

Maximum amount I am comfortable investing: $ _____

"I promise . . . to be realistic in terms of all financial aspects of this venture. I have a clear understanding of my net worth and my household monthly income and personal living expenses. I will not invest more than that amount which is financially responsible."

X _____   X _____

           Signature   **Date**

Step 4: Are You On The Right Path to Achieve Your Financial Vision?

PURPOSE

» Educate yourself on retirement planning by using your vision as the financial goal.

» Analyze your current path to determine if it will allow you to make your vision a reality.

» Understand the financial variance between your goals and your current path.

» Target strategies to improve your chances of reaching your financial goals.

Every vision can become reality. Unfortunately, most people never measure whether their current path will allow them to achieve their vision. Do you know if you are on the right path?

The following set of exercises will take a very complex mathematical formula and greatly simplify it. For example, we have not included the time value of money nor have we calculated the future values of potential Social Security income, if it still exists when you reach retirement age. This simplification is acceptable for the purpose of this workbook; however, we encourage you to learn more.

If you want to go through a more detailed financial analysis, there are a number of internet sites that will help you. Go to Google and type in the key words "retirement calculator." This will list hundreds of websites that can help. Some are simple and others complex. Or you can seek advice of a professional financial planner. The goal is to answer this question, "Am I currently on the path to financial independence?"

EXAMINE YOUR CURRENT PATH

It's time to examine your current path. Will your current path get you where you want to go? The following questions are designed to help you understand, in a very basic way, whether or not you are on track.

✎ EXERCISE 4.1: MY CURRENT PATH

1	**How old are you currently?**	years old
2	**How much have you saved for retirement?** *Add together the retirement and investment accounts found on page 20 along with other investments you will liquidate for retirement.*	$
3	**What are your Current Monthly Net Savings?** *See page 23.*	$
4	**What are your Annual Net Savings?** *Multiply total Current Monthly Net Savings (line 3) by 12 (months).*	$
5	**At what age do you intend to fully retire?** *This is the point at which you intend to fully dedicate yourself to other pursuits. Time with the grandchildren, golf, missionary work, etc.*	years old
6	**Once fully retired, how much after-tax money will you need on an annual basis to maintain your lifestyle?** *This can be found in Exercise 1.7, Cost of Your Vision (page 8).*	$
7	**To what age do you expect to live?** *For life expectancy tables search Google for "SSA Period Life Table." Adjust these tables based on the history of your family—genetics make a difference.*	years old
8	**What are your potential pre-retirement savings?** *Subtract line 1 (current age) from line 5 (retirement age) then multiply by line 4 (Annual Net Savings).*	$
9	**What are your current, expected lifetime savings?** *Add line 2 (current retirement savings) to line 8 (future retirement savings).*	$
10	**What is your total cost of retirement?** *Subtract line 5 (retirement age) from Line 7 (life expectancy) then multiply by line 6 (cost of retirement on an annual basis).*	$

COST OF YOUR VISION

What is the cost of your vision? Rewrite the annual cost of your vision below (see page 8).

Annual cost of my vision: _____

ARE YOU ON TRACK?

The exercise above has allowed you to compare the expected cost of retirement to your expected lifetime savings. Is the answer what you thought it would be? At this point you may want to think about a few additional questions:

Q: How confident are you in regard to preserving your income streams?

A: _____

Q: If you lose your job at age fifty-five, will you be able to secure another job with the same salary and benefits?

A: _____

Q: How confident are you in regard to controlling your expenses?

A: _____

Q: Do you believe your cost of living will increase or decrease?

A: _____

Q: Do you feel that you have sufficient margin of safety in your numbers to deal with the unexpected?

A: _____

If the verdict is not what you want or you are simply looking for additional margin of safety, you do have alternatives. Most people choose among the following options when they decide to take control of their financial future.

EXERCISE 4.2: MY STRATEGY TO TAKE CONTROL OF MY FINANCIAL FUTURE

Check the strategies you intend to utilize.

- [ ] **Work harder, get a raise, get a promotion, get a new job, and/or save more money. At the same time, reduce spending. Invest savings in the market—stocks or bonds are the normal alternatives.**

- [ ] **Invest in real-estate that should, over time, appreciate in value. Most people focus on residential properties and take a long-term approach to these types of investments.**

- [ ] **Build a business that is large enough to create passive or semi-passive income streams well into retirement years.**

- [ ] **Build a business that is large enough to eventually sell, creating a nest egg for retirement.**

These options are not exclusive of one another. Think about this: self-employed people make up less than 20% of the workers in America but account for two-thirds of the millionaires (*The Millionaire Next Door* by Stanley and Danko).

At this point, the goal is to get you thinking about what it will really take to achieve your financial goals. It is easy to say that you want something but quite another thing to take the required actions to achieve your goals. This is when most people start to waiver on their vision. It is simply easier to reduce your expectations than to take the required actions to achieve your dreams. What will you do? This is the first test.

"**I promise** . . . to not be only a dreamer. I promise to figure out what is financially needed to help me reach my dreams, goals, and vision. With this information in hand, I will be better equipped to identify the ideal franchise match that will take me where I want to go."

X _____   X _____

                     Signature   **Date**

Step 5: Assess Your Entrepreneurial Skills

"Time is limited, so I better wake up every morning fresh and know that I have just one chance to live this particular day right, and to string my days together into a life of action, and purpose."

~ Lance Armstrong (born September 18, 1971)
7-time winner of the Tour de France

PURPOSE

» **Learn about the common traits among successful entrepreneurs.**

» **Complete the Entrepreneurial Self-Assessment.**

By this time you may be coming to the realization that business ownership could be a viable path for you. Naturally you may wonder whether or not you have what it takes. That may sound like a daunting question. But that is the magic of franchising. It is not a mystery. There are folks with similar backgrounds, similar skill sets, and similar markets that have blazed the trail before you. If they can do it, so can you! If you are honest with your self-assessment and follow proper investigation steps, your confidence will rise and you will make a smart decision.

Over the years of working with scores of entrepreneurs, it has become clear that successful entrepreneurs do share certain traits. It is frustrating to see people in traditional employment with so many skills and amazing work ethic making others rich. We want to shake some sense into them: "Hey . . . open your eyes. What are you doing with your life? You have what it takes!"

It might surprise you to learn the shared traits among successful entrepreneurs.

COMMON TRAITS OF SUCCESSFUL ENTREPRENEURS

Trait # 1: Maintain a clear vision—both personally and for the business.

Trait # 2: Confidently communicate the vision and motivate others to action.

Trait # 3: Set timetables for achievement.

Trait # 4: View setbacks as learning opportunities.

Trait # 5: Feel comfortable standing apart from the crowd.

Trait # 6: Always focus on opportunities to learn.

Trait # 7: Assume accountability—never pass the buck.

Trait # 8: Believe in the importance of a positive attitude.

Trait # 9: Personally drive any situation until it works.

Trait #10: Take action—even when hurdles exist.

SELF-EVALUATION

For each of these common traits, rank yourself on a scale from 1 to 10 (with 1 being a clear weakness and 10 being a definite strength), using the following exercise. Please also write down an example of when you successfully exhibited each trait.

 A WORD TO THE WISE

Many people are looking for a test or an evaluation to tell them whether business ownership is right for them. Remember back to high school—you likely took a test that said you should be a fireman, farmer, or nurse. Well, since high school you have done many different jobs and you have probably done most of them successfully. This, and any other evaluation, must be taken with a grain of salt. No evaluation can truly predict your level of success. Evaluations are simply guideposts. There are many paths to success.

EXERCISE 5.1: ENTREPRENEURIAL SELF-ASSESSMENT

Trait #1: Maintain a clear vision—both personally and for the business.

"I have a clear vision and values. I am confident in my direction."

Weakness ⬅️ 1. 2. 3. 4. 5. 6. 7. 8. 9. 10 ➡️ Strength

Example: _____

_____

_____

Trait #2: Confidently communicate the vision and motivate others to action.

"Others listen and respond to what I say. I am a natural leader and others are drawn to me."

Weakness ⬅️ 1. 2. 3. 4. 5. 6. 7. 8. 9. 10 ➡️ Strength

Example: _____

_____

_____

Trait #3: Set timetables for achievement.

"I not only set goals to keep me focused, I set benchmarks for progress and timelines for implementation."

Weakness ⬅️ 1. 2. 3. 4. 5. 6. 7. 8. 9. 10 ➡️ Strength

Example: _____

_____

_____

Trait #4: View setbacks as learning opportunities.

"I believe setbacks are simply opportunities to learn, grow, and improve."

Weakness ⬅ 1. 2. 3. 4. 5. 6. 7. 8. 9. 10 ➡ Strength

Example: _____

_____

_____

Trait #5: Feel comfortable standing apart from the crowd.

"I am comfortable being uncommon in an all too common world."

Weakness ⬅ 1. 2. 3. 4. 5. 6. 7. 8. 9. 10 ➡ Strength

Example: _____

_____

_____

Trait #6: Always focus on opportunities to learn.

"I am a student of life. I surround myself with good teachers and seek out opportunities to learn."

Weakness ⬅ 1. 2. 3. 4. 5. 6. 7. 8. 9. 10 ➡ Strength

Example: _____

_____

_____

Trait #7: Assume accountability—never pass the buck.

"I own my successes and failures. Others know they can count on me and my word."

Weakness ⬅ 1. 2. 3. 4. 5. 6. 7. 8. 9. 10 ➡ Strength

Example: _____

_____

_____

Trait #8: Believe in the importance of a positive attitude.

"I am optimistic about myself and what my future holds."

Weakness ⬅ 1. 2. 3. 4. 5. 6. 7. 8. 9. 10 ➡ Strength

Example: _____

_____

_____

Trait #9: Personally drive any situation until it works.

"I am committed to setting a positive example, being financially successful, and running an extraordinary business."

Weakness ⬅ 1. 2. 3. 4. 5. 6. 7. 8. 9. 10 ➡ Strength

Example: _____

_____

_____

Trait #10: Take action—even when hurdles exist.

"No matter what happens, I always have a backup plan to get me to my goals. Setbacks simply give me an opportunity to exercise greater creativity."

Weakness ⬅ 1. 2. 3. 4. 5. 6. 7. 8. 9. 10 ➡ Strength

Example: _____

_____

_____

Add up your points. If you scored below a 30, you may need to be cautious about becoming an entrepreneur. If you scored between 30 and 60, you may be on the right path. If you scored over 60, you share the same characteristics of many successful entrepreneurs.

"I promise . . . I will be honest in my self-assessment. If I lack the basic traits displayed by successful entrepreneurs, I will focus my energies elsewhere. If I do share the common traits of successful entrepreneurs, I will proceed with confidence, determination, and an open mind."

X _____ X _____

Signature   **Date**

Step 6: Establish Your Business and Lifestyle Profiles

"The key is you have to have the guts to go for it."

~ Tony Robbins (born February 29, 1960)
American self-help writer and professional speaker

PURPOSE

» Identify your key strengths and skills.

» Analyze your lead generation and sales profile.

» Analyze your employee management profile.

» Contemplate, define, and prioritize your lifestyle requirements and goals.

Has anyone given you the advice, "Do what you love!"? A better mantra would be, "Do what you are good at!" If you speak to ten successful entrepreneurs, you will find the product or service almost becomes incidental. Successful entrepreneurs love building businesses. Learn to be like them and make being a successful business owner your primary objective. Successful entrepreneurs leverage their core competencies while being passionate about business ownership. If you can do this you have unlocked the combination for success.

ASSESS YOUR STRENGTHS AND SKILLS

When you call and interview franchisees, ask them, "What traits do the most successful franchise owners have in common?" Ideally, they will answer with some of your top strengths and skills. Otherwise you will need to focus attention elsewhere. Playing to your strengths and skills is key to a successful match.

EXERCISE 6.1: MY BUSINESS SKILLS

Rank your ability in regard to each of the following fifteen skills. Your strongest ability should be ranked number 1. Your second strongest ability should be ranked number 2 and so on until you reach your weakest area, which would be ranked number 15.

	Rank (strongest = 1)
Real estate (site selection, lease negotiations)	_____
Marketing and advertising	_____
Public relations	_____
Networking and community involvement	_____
Public speaking	_____
Proactive sales (approaching new customers)	_____
Reactive sales (responding to interested people)	_____
Customer service	_____
Training staff	_____
Managing staff	_____
Technical skills (programming, engineering, architecture, design)	_____
Supplier relationships (identification and negotiations)	_____
Finance (debt, equity, cash-flow analysis)	_____
Accounting (external reporting, taxes)	_____
Legal (licensing, business formation, permits, labor laws)	_____

In order to maximize your potential for success it is important to maximize the connection between your skills and the requirements of the business. In most cases your top three skills will be the ones you focus on. In some cases a prospective franchisee wishes to move away from a certain skill. If this is the case, then choose the next strongest skill.

> **What are your three main skills you want to leverage in building and operating your new business?**
>
> 1: _____   2: _____   3: _____

Also recognize the skills you do not have. Carefully check the franchisor's support systems in those areas to make sure they can help you in areas of inexperience or weakness. Typically, those starting their first business do not have the skills and knowledge to make it a success alone. That is why it is smart to focus on a franchise. Successful entrepreneurs build their knowledge base in order to evolve into more sophisticated, independent entrepreneurs. But, we all have to start somewhere.

What are my three biggest weaknesses? In which areas is it critical for me to have exceptional advisors and support?

1: _____ 2: _____ 3: _____

DISCOVER YOUR BUSINESS PROFILE

One key area to carefully examine is your comfort level with lead generation and sales. It's easy to imagine a business where you put up your sign, open the doors, and the customers come flooding in. The reality is not that simple. Successful entrepreneurs make it look easy, but even businesses with the most built-in customer demand require constant networking, sales, and promotion.

Think about lead generation in two ways. One is proactive and the other is reactive. Proactive marketing involves reaching out to the customers and driving them to your business. Reactive marketing involves putting materials in the marketplace and waiting for the customer to come to you. Someone who is very social would quickly get frustrated in a business that required them to sit behind a counter and wait for the customers to show up. Someone who is naturally shy would quickly get frustrated in a business that required them to go out and find customers. Marketing drives lead generation. Sales is about converting that lead into a paying customer.

Think about your preference for generating leads and sales. Do you prefer to be reactive, proactive, or somewhere in the middle?

"To create a new business that makes money, and more significantly, employs others, and more significantly, gives a product to a customer that improves their life, is our greatest challenge, our greatest opportunity, and the greatest gift, far greater than any charity that we can give our fellow person."

—Paul Zane Pilzer (born 1954), economist, entrepreneur, and author

✏️ EXERCISE 6.2: CUSTOMER ACQUISITION

Read and score each of these statements:

	NOT A MATCH	POOR MATCH	POSSIBLE MATCH	DEFINITE MATCH
I am very proactive when it comes to getting new customers. If I do not have a customer in front of me, I am going to go out and create one.	1	2	3	4
I do not necessarily like to sell, but I am very social. I have a wide network of friends and I am a good networker.	1	2	3	4
I enjoy sales but do not want to hunt for new customers. I would rather have a marketing program that drives customers to me. Then I would enjoy engaging in a discussion regarding my service or product.	1	2	3	4
I don't really like to sell. The ideal business would be one where a marketing program drives people to me and I would answer their questions.	1	2	3	4

🍎 NOTES

_____

_____

_____

_____

_____

_____

✎ EXERCISE 6.3: CUSTOMER RELATIONSHIPS

Do you have a preference for the type of customer with whom you'll interact? Identify which categories are most attractive to you.

Read and score each of these statements:

	NOT A MATCH	POOR MATCH	POSSIBLE MATCH	DEFINITE MATCH
I prefer selling to and servicing other businesses. Business-to-business relationships are the most comfortable for me.	1	2	3	4
I prefer selling to and servicing consumers. Business-to-consumer relationships are the most comfortable for me.	1	2	3	4
I prefer quick transactional sales, like selling a sandwich at Subway® or a can of Coke® in a convenience store.	1	2	3	4
I prefer a business where I get to know the customer on a personal level.	1	2	3	4
I like a one-time hit. In and out, with a high-ticket sale.	1	2	3	4
I like recurring sales. Once I gain a new customer, I want to keep that customer for as long as possible and service them on a regular basis.	1	2	3	4

🍎 NOTES

_____

_____

_____

_____

_____

EXERCISE 6.4: EMPLOYEE BACKGROUNDS

To be well-matched to your opportunity, ask yourself who you would best manage? Who would you enjoy managing the most?

Read and score each of these statements:

	NOT A MATCH	POOR MATCH	POSSIBLE MATCH	DEFINITE MATCH
I am more effective at managing blue-collar individuals.	1	2	3	4
I am more effective at managing white-collar individuals.	1	2	3	4
I am more effective at managing educated individuals.	1	2	3	4
I am more effective at managing skilled individuals.	1	2	3	4
I am more effective at managing unskilled individuals.	1	2	3	4
Education level does not matter. I work well with all people.	1	2	3	4
I am more effective at managing mature individuals.	1	2	3	4
I am more effective at managing males.	1	2	3	4
I am more effective at managing females.	1	2	3	4

I am more effective at managing in a high-turnover environment. I gain comfort in knowing that these individuals are easy to replace, if needed. They cannot hold me hostage.	1	2	3	4
I am more effective at managing in a low-turnover environment. I like the fact that these individuals are likely to show up for work; if they quit, I know replacing them will take time and effort.	1	2	3	4

✏ EXERCISE 6.5: EMPLOYEE NUMBERS

Now that you have thought about the backgrounds you would be most effective managing, give some consideration to the ideal team size. Which description best suits your goals?

Read and score each of these statements:

	NOT A MATCH	POOR MATCH	POSSIBLE MATCH	DEFINITE MATCH
I prefer to begin as an owner/operator business and remain that way.	1	2	3	4
I prefer to begin as an owner/operator business and then add a small team as the business grows.	1	2	3	4
I prefer to start with a small team of employees and then grow as needed.	1	2	3	4
I am good at and enjoy managing employees. I would be happy with a large group of employees.	1	2	3	4

Keep this data top-of-mind when you get to the stage of picking potential target franchises. This information is critical not only for achieving success but it is also essential for your satisfaction level.

EXERCISE 6.6: FRANCHISE CULTURE

Every franchise, as with every organization, has its own personality. Think about how the right franchise will feel. As you progress through each investigation, it is important that you experience an emotional connection with the franchise owners, the management team, and the employees. Simply put, it should feel like home.

Circle the key words that help you "feel at home."

Honesty	Mature	Unrestrictive	Integrity
Strict	Persistent	Technology-oriented	Strong vision
First to market	Faith-based	Dominant	Inclusive
Professional environment	Passionate	Determined	Analytical
Clarity of purpose	Laidback	Innovative	Assertive
Driven	Team-oriented	Competitive	Easy-going
Serious	Lean	Flexible	Entrepreneurial
Fun	Fast-paced	Passive	Family-oriented
Creative	Transparency	Steady	Conservative

How else will you know that you have found a franchise home? What are you looking for from the ideal franchise partner?

_____

_____

_____

_____

DISCOVER YOUR LIFESTYLE PROFILE

We find that when working with prospective franchisees they often arrive with a specific business in mind. But starting the search with a specific franchise product or service in mind is backwards and leads to poor choices. This is analogous to the tail wagging the dog. You can pick the business and adjust to meet the needs of the business or you can define your needs and goals first, picking the business that best fits you.

So how do you want to live your life? These exercises will help you think through and clarify important lifestyle issues. Dare to dream! You really can have it all!

EXERCISE 6.7: BUSINESS LOCATION

There are several types of locations from which your business can operate. Which business location would you enjoy the most? Which business location best meets your lifestyle goals?

Read and score each of these statements:

	NOT A MATCH	POOR MATCH	POSSIBLE MATCH	DEFINITE MATCH
I prefer a retail-based business that works out of a storefront.	1	2	3	4
Working out of a warehouse, workshop, or garage fits me best.	1	2	3	4
I prefer a business operating out of a traditional office space.	1	2	3	4
The ideal business is one where my office is at home and I go to see my customers or clients.	1	2	3	4

NOTES

_____

_____

_____

_____

_____

_____

EXERCISE 6.8: WORK ENVIRONMENT

If you have not enjoyed cubical life, you may want to look for options where you can be out-and-about during the course of the day. If you enjoy having one place to go and you like to "stay put," a business that has you behind a desk or a counter may be the best fit. What is your ideal work environment?

Read and score these statements:

	NOT A MATCH	POOR MATCH	POSSIBLE MATCH	DEFINITE MATCH
I enjoy being out-and-about, where every day is different and I am constantly stimulated.	1	2	3	4
I prefer to stay in one location all day. I believe this will allow me to be focused and more efficient.	1	2	3	4

EXERCISE 6.9: DRESS CODE

We want you to be comfortable in your environment. A business where you need to wear a suit every day has a different feel than a business where you dress informally. What is your preference?

Read and score these statements:

	NOT A MATCH	POOR MATCH	POSSIBLE MATCH	DEFINITE MATCH
I feel most comfortable in a suit. I like to look sharp and professional.	1	2	3	4
I prefer business casual.	1	2	3	4
I prefer casual dress.	1	2	3	4
If I could work in my bath robe, I would be ecstatic.	1	2	3	4

EXERCISE 6.10: OPERATIONAL COMPLEXITY

How much complexity are you looking for in your day? Some people prefer options that are operationally simple; others prefer options that are operationally complex. Which option do you prefer?

Read and score these statements:

	NOT A MATCH	POOR MATCH	POSSIBLE MATCH	DEFINITE MATCH
I believe that the best business is a simple business.	1	2	3	4
Although simple businesses may be nice, I really need a business that will keep me intellectually stimulated. A complex business will give me the challenge I need.	1	2	3	4

EXERCISE 6.11: SOCIAL STATUS

Do you care what other people think about what you are doing for a living? Are you status-conscious? Could you own a service company where your employees clean public restrooms and still hold your head up high? Read that question again. It says where your employees clean restrooms, not you. Do not get the task of the business confused with the tasks of the owner, unless you seek a business that does not have employees. What if that business met all of your financial and lifestyle goals? Is status an issue for you?

Read and score these statements:

	NOT A MATCH	POOR MATCH	POSSIBLE MATCH	DEFINITE MATCH
Status is very important. I would have a hard time speaking to family or friends about the business unless the business sounds impressive.	1	2	3	4
Status is somewhat important. I would like an impressive business but I am open to moderate status businesses for the right return.	1	2	3	4
Status makes no difference to me. I could be happy with a business that picked up dog refuse so long as it met my other goals.	1	2	3	4

EXERCISE 6.12: GOOD WILL

More and more individuals want work to sustain them and to provide them with the ability to make a positive difference in the world. Is that important to you?

Read and score these statements:

	NOT A MATCH	POOR MATCH	POSSIBLE MATCH	DEFINITE MATCH
I am willing to sacrifice flexibility and return if I am able to help directly improve the lives of others through my product or service.	1	2	3	4
I am interested in "doing good," not just making money. But, I do realize "doing good" can simply mean being a good employer, being a good member of the community, and providing good customer service.	1	2	3	4
A strong return-on-investment and a flexible lifestyle are important to me. As long as the business is not immoral or unethical, it does not matter what my product or service is. If I have the time and money, I can contribute to noble causes on my own.	1	2	3	4

NOTES

_____

_____

_____

_____

_____

_____

✎ EXERCISE 6.13: PASSION

We have all heard it: "Do what you love and the money will follow." But in working with experienced entrepreneurs we know that their first passion is building and managing a successful business. Occasionally prospective entrepreneurs try to turn their hobbies into a business but this is not the common path used by the most successful entrepreneurs. If you need more information on this topic, reread chapter 4 of *The Educated Franchisee* before answering the questions below.

Read and score each of these statements:

	NOT A MATCH	POOR MATCH	POSSIBLE MATCH	DEFINITE MATCH
The business must connect to my hobbies or interests. I am willing to sacrifice flexibility and income to meet this goal.	1	2	3	4
The business needs to meet my lifestyle and income goals. It is not overly important for the business to connect to my hobbies or interests. I can pursue my hobbies, passions, and interests on my own time.	1	2	3	4
My passion is building a business. The service or widget is incidental, as long as I can reach my other goals.	1	2	3	4

🍎 NOTES

_____

_____

_____

_____

_____

_____

✎ EXERCISE 6.14: FOCUS

According to Franchise Disclosure Documents, approximately 80% of franchised businesses require the full-time commitment of the franchisee. This means that it is not acceptable to maintain a job and start the business on the side. The advantage of full-time entry is that you typically can reach the break-even point more quickly.

Approximately 20% of businesses allow for part-time focus. If you want to consider part-time options, it is important to remember that the business is still a full-time enterprise. Therefore, you will have to pay a manager a fair wage—money that would otherwise go to you. Part-time entry will delay your cash-flow break-even point, but will provide added security because you can maintain your current employment and income stream.

Part-time commitment to the business only works when you have significant work flexibility. If there is an issue with the business during the day, you need to be able to address the issue without upsetting your boss. What time commitment is right for you?

Read and score these statements:

	NOT A MATCH	POOR MATCH	POSSIBLE MATCH	DEFINITE MATCH
Even though I am employed, in the perfect world I would leave my current employer and commit to the business full time.	1	2	3	4
I am not currently employed and I am only interested in full-time businesses that can support my family.	1	2	3	4
I am currently employed and prefer to stay in my current position while the business grows. I have the flexibility to handle any issues that may arise. I am aware that this significantly reduces my options and will delay my break-even point.	1	2	3	4
I would like to examine full-time and part-time entry options. The critical factors will be break-even averages and financial viability.	1	2	3	4

EXERCISE 6.15: TIME COMMITMENT

If you focus on full-time entry options, keep your work/life balance needs in mind. Balance is an important issue for many would-be franchise owners. Determine what hours you want to put into the business per week. You should expect most businesses to be "front-end loaded." This means that you are unlikely, with almost any business, to enjoy much work/life balance before the business reaches the break-even point. What hours will work best for you?

Read and score these statements:

	NOT A MATCH	POOR MATCH	POSSIBLE MATCH	DEFINITE MATCH
I will work as many hours as needed in the first year. I will do whatever is needed to be successful.	1	2	3	4
I will work very hard during the first year, but I also need a little time off each week.	1	2	3	4
The ideal business would require my attention Monday through Friday, with limited evening and weekend commitments.	1	2	3	4
It is important that I am able to balance work and play. I will give up income if it means more time with family and friends.	1	2	3	4
Family comes first. The hours of the business must revolve around family and pleasure.	1	2	3	4

EXERCISE 6.16: FLEXIBILITY

Do you mind if the business controls your schedule? Or do you want to control the hours you focus on the business? Another way to look at this: How important is flexibility in your work day?

Read and score these statements:

	NOT A MATCH	POOR MATCH	POSSIBLE MATCH	DEFINITE MATCH
I am most comfortable in a business that has set hours each day. This way I have a fixed work schedule.	1	2	3	4
Set hours for the business is okay, but I also want some flexibility to adjust the schedule, if needed.	1	2	3	4
Flexibility is important to me. I understand that most businesses have normal hours, but I also need to be able to schedule other things into my day, as needed.	1	2	3	4
I really dislike schedules and do not like to be tied down. I am okay with significant hours, but I need to have full control over which hours I work.	1	2	3	4

At this point you have firmly outlined many of your most important lifestyle requirements. Are there any other lifestyle goals and requirements that are important to you? If so, list them here.

_____

_____

_____

_____

_____

_____

_____

_____

✎ EXERCISE 6.17: PRIORITIZATION

Exercises 6.7 through 6.16 focus on important lifestyle goals. Even though you may have an opinion on each of these subjects, some of them will seem more important than the others. In your search for the perfect business it is hard to find 100% of everything you want; therefore, it is important to prioritize.

In this last exercise, please review exercises 6.7 through 6.16 and rank each subject in regard to importance. The most important should be ranked number 1. The second most important should be ranked number 2 and so on until you reach the least important, which would be ranked number 10.

	RANK
Business Location	
Work Environment	
Dress Code	
Operational Complexity	
Social Status	
Good Will	
Passion	
Focus	
Time Commitment	
Flexibility	

Finding a business that meets your income goals is smart; finding a business that meets your skills, and business and lifestyle goals, that's priceless!

"**I promise**... to focus on options that play to my strengths and that matches my sales, management, and culture profiles. I will also remember that my goal is not only to be a business owner. My goal is to be a business owner, living the lifestyle I desire and that I design. I understand that if I focus on return, not only in terms of financial return but also in terms of lifestyle, my return can be invaluable."

X _____   X _____

<table>
<tr><td align="center">Signature</td><td align="center">Date</td></tr>
</table>

Step 7: Determine Your Financial Goals

"To accomplish great things we must not only act but also dream; not only plan, but also believe."

~ Author Unknown

PURPOSE

» **Define your first-year income goal.**

» **Plan a strategy to cover your first-year living expenses.**

» **Define your long-term income and wealth-creation goals.**

» **Understand and calculate the business asset value based on income goals.**

Before you begin to identify potential franchise matches, you need to clearly define your financial return needs and goals.

The exercises in step 3 helped you understand where you are now in regard to net worth, household cash flow, and maximum investment. The exercises in step 4 helped you translate your vision into a dollar amount, determine the total cost of your retirement, and evaluate if you are on track. This step is focused on setting minimum financial requirements that your target business must surpass in order to be financially viable and financially attractive.

In order to get the best results, please read chapter 5 of *The Educated Franchisee*. The information in chapter 5 will help you fully understand the less obvious but very real financial benefits of entrepreneurship over being an employee.

DEFINE FIRST-YEAR INCOME GOAL

The first year in any business is financially challenging; however, by now you understand entrepreneurship is not about short-term gain, it is about long-term wealth creation and personal freedom. Will you be able to take money out of the business in the first year? Maybe. But for this exercise, let's assume that you choose not to pull any money out of the business in year one. Instead, you reinvest the profits back into the future growth of the business. If you assume this, then it is necessary to determine how you will cover your first-year living expenses.

EXERCISE 7.1: ADJUSTED ANNUAL LIVING EXPENSE

1	Refer back to page 23. What is your current monthly net savings? (*See page 23, exercise 3.4.*)	$
2	If one spouse quits their job to run the business full time, what will be your adjusted monthly net savings? (Subtract reduced income from line 1. Note: this may be a negative amount.)	$
3	Consider ways to increase your monthly income. • Spouse gets a job • Collect debts that people owe you • Other What additional monthly income can you generate?	$
4	Adjusted monthly net income (add line 2 to line 3).	$
5	Current monthly expenses. (*See page 22–23.*)	$
6	Reduce monthly expenses. • Eliminate retirement contributions for one year • Decrease the amount of times you dine out • Forgo your cleaning or yard service • Consolidate your debt • Transfer personal expenses into business expenses (phone, internet, etc.) • Other What monthly expenses can you reduce?	$
7	Adjusted monthly expenses (line 5 minus line 6).	$
8	Adjusted monthly net savings (line 4 minus line 7)?	$
9	Multiply the adjusted monthly net cash flow by 12 months. This is your adjusted annual living expense. (Note: this may be a negative number.)	$

STRATEGIES TO COVER FIRST-YEAR PERSONAL EXPENSES

If the adjusted annual living expense is zero or positive, then you may be in a stable position and will not have to worry about covering your first-year living expenses.

If you find that your income is not sufficient to cover your personal expenses, then you will have a negative personal cash flow in the first year. You need to ensure that you are financially positioned to cover your living expenses. There are three strategies to make this happen. The three main strategies are as follows:

STRATEGY 1

Find a franchise that can create a fast positive cash flow—within nine, six, or even three months. This is possible, and probably a good thing to aim for, but income is never guaranteed. While faster positive cash flow may happen, it is probably best to assume you will not take any money out in the first year.

STRATEGY 2

Overfund your business. As you explore finance options, understand it is often possible to include personal cash flow needs in the loan application. If you need an extra $36,000 to cover your living expenses, you can add $36,000 to your loan application, Home Equity Line of Credit (HELOC), or to your Rollover for Business Start-up (ROBS) program. This will allow you to pay yourself a salary in the first year due to the overfunding.

STRATEGY 3

Reduce your maximum investment amount by the amount needed to cover your personal cash-flow needs. If your maximum investment amount is $200,000 but you need $50,000 to cover your personal living expenses, your new maximum investment amount would be $150,000. The extra $50,000 would remain in the business account to cover your first-year personal income needs.

My strategy to cover first-year living expenses is . . . _____

_____

_____

_____

_____

_____

_____

_____

_____

_____

LONG-TERM INCOME AND WEALTH-CREATION GOALS

Obviously the objective of entrepreneurship is to create strong positive cash flow, build an asset of tremendous value, and reduce taxes.

How much money will it take to achieve the goals you have set for yourself? Rewrite these numbers here:

Annual cost of vision: _____ (page 8)

Expected lifetime cost of retirement: _____ (page 28—line 10)

Focus on these numbers. If you know your financial goals, you have a much better chance of reaching them. You need to create a financial game plan to achieve your objectives and then find a business that will get you there.

Use all of the resources at your disposal to define your net income goals for year one, year two, year three, and beyond. It is important to discuss these goals with your spouse or significant other and make sure they agree with you and share these goals.

EXERCISE 7.3: NET INCOME GOALS

Write your annual net income goals here.

	NET INCOME GOALS/ OWNER BENEFIT
Year 1	
Year 2	
Year 3	
Year 4	
Year 5	
Final year prior to selling	

VALUATION OF YOUR BUSINESS

It is important that you understand the true value of business ownership. You need to learn to think like an entrepreneur not an employee. As an employee, it is fairly simple to understand the financial benefits of a salary. As a business owner, it is not just about owner benefit or what you draw out of the business. It is also about creation of an asset that YOU own.

Business valuation is subject to a large number of variables. At the risk of over-simplification, valuation of your business is based on a multiple of earnings (earnings are also referred to as "owner benefit"). Although each industry and each business will potentially sell at a different multiple of earnings, historically most healthy, profitable businesses sell for between two and a half to four times owner benefit. Here is a conservative example to help you understand the asset creation piece of entrepreneurship.

Example: Asset Value

	OWNER BENEFIT		ASSET VALUE
Year 1	$25,000	× 2.5	$62,500
Year 2	$50,000	× 2.5	$125,000
Year 3	$100,000	× 2.5	$250,000
Year 4	$200,000	× 2.5	$500,000
Year 5	$400,000	× 2.5	$1,000,000
Year 10	$500,000	× 2.5	$1,250,000

EXERCISE 7.4: ASSET VALUE PROJECTION

The next step is to value the business you want to create. Take the net owner benefit in the final year prior to selling and enter the projection here (see page 59).

_____ × 2.5 = _____

Net owner benefit for the final year prior to selling   **Projected resale value**

If you work backwards from owner benefit and asset value, you should be able to set reasonable objectives for the performance of the business in order to achieve your financial objectives and, as a result, your goals and vision.

As a business owner you also have certain tax benefits. These benefits change from year to year but it is safe to say that business owners are legally able to pay less tax and, regardless of how the laws may change, this is likely to remain the case in years to come. Reread chapter 12 in *The Educated Franchisee* to get a better sense of the basics. If you want a more detailed review of the tax advantages of business ownership, read *Loopholes of the Rich*, by Diane Kennedy.

It is also important to remember that you do not have to achieve all of your financial goals with one business. Once you become a business owner, there is a good chance that you will own more than one business in the years to come.

"**I understand** . . . life is about choices. A successful life is about making smart, informed choices. I can live life in the proverbial pinball machine—bouncing around at the will of others—or I can create my own destiny, my own asset, and reach my own financial goals."

X _____ X _____

Signature   **Date**

Step 8: Identify the Best Franchises to Investigate

"If you wait for opportunities to occur, you will be one of the crowd."

~ Edward de Bono (born 1933)
Physician, author, and inventor

PURPOSE

» **Determine if you want to work with a franchise consultant.**

» **If yes, find a consultant with experience, expertise, and ethics.**

» **Use key criteria to identify target franchises.**

» **Check territory availability of target franchises.**

» **Enter the franchise investigations void of preconceived notions.**

Progress! You have clearly defined key criteria to help you identify the ideal franchise match, including: vision, net worth, maximum investment, cost of your vision, strengths and skills, lead generation and sales profile, employee management profile, franchise culture profile, lifestyle goals, as well as short-term, long-term, and wealth-creation goals.

Having a clear picture of where you want to go is the key to opening the door to a more vibrant and fulfilling future. Now it is time to pick your targets, to set your sights. Be prepared, this is one of the most challenging steps in the process.

Did you know that there are more than 2,500 franchise options in over 90 distinct industries? How do you focus? This step is designed to help you do just that, to identify companies that are worth further consideration. There are two paths you can take.

UTILIZE A FRANCHISE CONSULTANT

Many people choose to work with a franchise consultant to help them with this crucial step. A quality franchise consultant is an individual with exceptional franchise and business ownership experience, whose full-time job is to study franchise opportunities and then introduce you, the potential franchisee, to them. Once the introduction is made, a quality consultant will guide you through the due-diligence process. Franchise consultants are paid by franchisors and are functionally similar to executive recruiters or buyer's agents in a real estate transaction. A high-quality franchise consultant will save you an enormous amount of time and can create a win-win situation for all involved.

🦉 A WORD TO THE WISE

Unfortunately, not all franchise consultants are experienced in business ownership and/or franchising. There are no regulations in regard to who can hang their shingle and claim to be a franchise consultant. It is up to you to interview prospective franchise consultants and make sure that you work with a truly knowledgeable individual.

Step one is to identify a respected franchise consulting firm. You can do this by going to http://www.educatedfranchisee.com/franchise-consulting-organizations.aspx. This page will give you criteria to help you choose a quality organization; it also recommends reputable franchise consulting organizations.

Step two is to interview the individual consultant to gauge their level of experience and expertise. Prior to contacting consultants, review chapter 14: "The Use of Outside Experts," in The Educated Franchisee, to make sure you are clear in regard to the ground rules for choosing a quality advisor.

A quality franchise consultant saves you time by helping you focus on proven franchise systems that are available in your area and that match your skills, abilities, needs, and desires. If you need help finding a great franchise consultant, contact us at info@educatedfranchisee.com. Do not settle until you find a trustworthy consultant with the right expertise, experience, ethics, and work style. They will become a key ally in your search for your future business.

"Do not wait; the time will never be 'just right.' Start where you stand, and work with whatever tools you may have at your command, and better tools will be found as you go along."

—Napoleon Hill (1883–1970), author of personal-success literature

✏️ EXERCISE 8.1: FRANCHISE CONSULTANT EVALUATION

Use the following form to record the name, contact information, and experience of the franchise consultant you select.

CONTACT INFORMATION

Consultant firm: _____   Consultant firm website: _____

Consultant name: _____   Consultant telephone #: _____

Consultant mobile #: _____   Consultant email: _____

EXPERIENCE

of years in franchising: _____

# of years as a franchise consultant: _____

Experience as a business owner and/or business leader: _____

Results of Google or Yahoo search on consultant: _____

Reviewed consultants biography: Yes / No

General summary of consultant's experience:

_____

_____

_____

_____

_____

_____

Once you identify a consultant, share the information from this workbook. This will help the consultant do their job. Experienced consultants will never just throw a bunch of franchise companies at you and see what sticks. They want to get to know you before they begin to suggest any franchise organizations. They develop a clear profile for your ideal franchise fit and make recommendations based on your criteria. The data in this workbook is invaluable in helping them do their job, so fax or scan and email them pertinent information.

GO IT ALONE

Not everyone is comfortable using a consultant. This is a matter of choice. If you were to purchase a home, would you do your own research—figure out which homes are for sale, how many bedrooms and bathrooms they have, etc.—and negotiate the purchase price directly? Does "For Sale By Owner" get your juices going because you believe you are better qualified to find the right deal than a real estate buyer's agent? If so, you may want to search for franchise opportunities without assistance.

If you choose to "go it alone" you should begin by using the internet to select your targets. Go to https://educatedfranchisee.com/resources/franchise-opportunites to find a list of reputable franchising websites. These websites allow you to sort options based on investment parameters and other basic criteria. Once you begin to focus on options that fit your investment requirements, you will find additional information to further sort. Net worth requirement, number of locations, and average number of employees are frequently detailed on franchise websites.

Websites typically do not say whether the franchise has availability and/or wants to grow in your target market. Additionally, websites make no representation as to whether the franchise system is successful. These websites are driven by advertising dollars. The more money the franchisor spends, the more likely the franchise will be rated as "Great," "Prime," or "Hot." So, in order to identify a few good opportunities, you need to begin with a fairly large list of options. Contact each company on your list, make it past the gatekeeper at the front desk, and reach someone who can answer your initial screening questions; then evaluate their answers.

Doing this on your own or with the assistance of a franchise consultant leads to two very different experiences. Which path is right for you? Only you can say.

INITIAL FRANCHISE SCREEN

To maximize efficiency, review some of the criteria you have developed for choosing a franchise. By cross-referencing your information with the information found on the websites, you will be able to drop the companies that are obviously not a good match for you. Those companies you are interested in should match the following criteria:

EXERCISE 8.2: FRANCHISE CRITERIA

Franchises that I qualify for have a net worth requirement at/below (see page 20):

_____

Total investment I'm willing to make is at/below (see page 25):

_____

The franchises will allow me to generate customers using the following approaches (see page 40):

_____

The franchise will allow me to employ individuals with the following backgrounds (see page 42):

_____

The franchise will, on average, employ the following number of employees (see page 43):

_____

The franchises will operate from the following locations (see page 45):

_____

EXERCISE 8.3: FRANCHISE SELECTION BASED ON CRITERIA

List the franchises that you want to research to see if they meet the above criteria. Continue the process on-line until you have identified ten potential franchises that meet the above criteria.

POTENTIAL FRANCHISE TARGETS	MEETS INITIAL CRITERIA
1. _____	Y/N
2. _____	Y/N
3. _____	Y/N
4. _____	Y/N
5. _____	Y/N
6. _____	Y/N
7. _____	Y/N
8. _____	Y/N
9. _____	Y/N
10. _____	Y/N

TERRITORY AVAILABILITY

If you are not using a consultant, you need to call each of the target franchisors to see if the territory you want is available. If you use email, be prepared to wait for answers. High-growth franchises can receive hundreds of inquiries each week. It speeds things up to call the Franchise Development Departments directly. Use the chart below to track territory availability. If you are using a consultant, your consultant will take care of the availability issues for you.

EXERCISE 8.4: FRANCHISE SELECTION BASED ON TERRITORY AVAILABILITY

List your potential target franchises and inquire if your market is available.

POTENTIAL FRANCHISE TARGETS	MEETS INITIAL CRITERIA
1. _____	Y/N
2. _____	Y/N
3. _____	Y/N
4. _____	Y/N
5. _____	Y/N
6. _____	Y/N
7. _____	Y/N
8. _____	Y/N
9. _____	Y/N
10. _____	Y/N

✎ EXERCISE 8.5: MY TOP THREE OPTIONS

Once the initial screens and territory checks are completed, list the top three options that you would like to focus on for in-depth investigations.

NAME OF FRANCHISE	FRANCHISE WEBSITE	FRANCHISE CONTACT NUMBER

It is important to have targets and focus; otherwise, you may struggle and ultimately be overwhelmed with the amount of options and information available. If you are not using a consultant, you might find it difficult to determine the true business characteristics of each franchise at this early stage. You might decide to add additional targets. Continue this process until you have three solid targets that want to expand in your market and meet your initial screening criteria.

Take a deep breath. The process of finding an ideal match is just taking shape. You know where you are headed. It is critical that you now clear your mind of preconceived notions. Three franchise names on a page do not equate to becoming a franchise owner. But be prepared, having three names on paper will get the average person's mind racing. When you commit a name to paper, you are only committing to research, not purchase. Do not get ahead of yourself. This is a life-changing process and requires significant due diligence. If you over think things right now and allow yourself to become overtaken by anxiety, you will never become a franchisee. Think back to our second step on fear. Remember courage is not the absence of fear, only the realization that something else is more important.

"I promise ... to pick my targets using a systematic approach, using initial screening criteria that is well thought out. I promise to not make decisions based on pre-conceived notions. I will dig in, gather the facts, and make an informed, educated, and courageous decision."

X _____   X _____

           Signature   **Date**

Step 9: Begin Your Investigations and Review FDDs

"It often requires more courage to dare to do right than to fear to do wrong."

~ Abraham Lincoln (1809-1865)
16th President of the United States

PURPOSE

» **Establish a timeline for your investigation process.**

» **Successfully initiate contact with target franchisors.**

» **Establish a strong foundation to begin your investigations.**

» **Review the Franchise Disclosure Documents (FDD).**

» **Identify questions and concerns raised while reviewing the FDD.**

» **Track key comparison data found in the Franchise Disclosure Documents.**

To bring about change—smart change—one needs to be committed. Contemplation does not equal commitment, just as desire does not equate to drive. Proper research of a franchise opportunity requires commitment. It is premature to commit to franchise ownership, but it is not premature to commit to a serious, focused investigation.

SET YOUR INVESTIGATION TIMEFRAME

So where does an investigation begin? It begins with commitment and timelines. Your commitment is to give your time and energy to discover if entrepreneurship is an ideal path for you in a specified time period. Remember, time and energy is an outward sign of drive. Successful entrepreneurs are driven people.

A proper franchise investigation is made up of finite steps. When investigating three options, proper due diligence will take about forty hours of time. Are you willing to commit forty hours?

How many weeks will this take? That depends on how many hours per week you have to put into a proper investigation. If you are not able to come up with a minimum of five hours per week, you need to:

1. Change your priorities and clear time in your schedule, or

2. Put the investigations on hold until you can commit to five hours per week, minimum.

🦉 A WORD TO THE WISE

Franchisors look for individuals who are focused and decisive. Being on a different timeframe than the franchisor can be construed as a lack of interest, lack of focus, or lack of decisiveness.

✏ EXERCISE 9.1: MY TIMEFRAME

How many hours per week will you put into investigations? _____

40 hours divided by _____ hours per week = _____ weeks.

Today's date: _____

Goal date for completion of investigations: _____

Does forty hours to investigate a franchise surprise you? As you immerse yourself in the due-diligence process, you may find your mind working overtime, putting in more than forty hours. But the "meat and potatoes" of a well-organized investigation should not take more than forty hours.

Most due-diligence timeframes are set between four to eight weeks. If your goal is to make a decision in six weeks, the following example reveals how your due diligence may progress. Use this chart to track your progress and to stay focused and accountable.

"My will shall shape my future. Whether I fail or succeed shall be no man's doing but my own. I am the force; I can clear any obstacle before me or I can be lost in the maze. My choice; my responsibility; win or lose, only I hold the key to my destiny."

—Elaine Maxwell, consultant and business coach

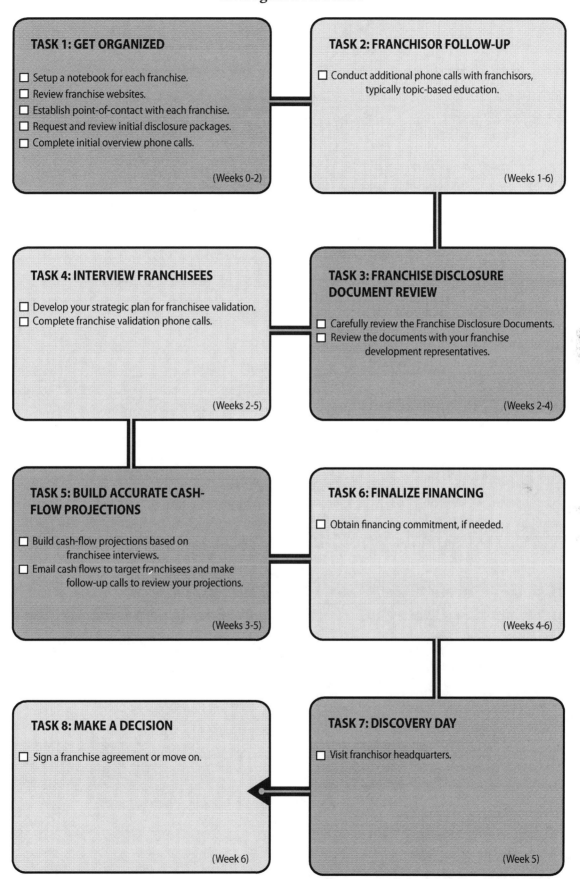

TASK 1: GET ORGANIZED

☐ Setup a notebook for each franchise.
☐ Review franchise websites.
☐ Establish point-of-contact with each franchise.
☐ Request and review initial disclosure packages.
☐ Complete initial overview phone calls.

(Weeks 0-2)

TASK 2: FRANCHISOR FOLLOW-UP

☐ Conduct additional phone calls with franchisors, typically topic-based education.

(Weeks 1-6)

TASK 4: INTERVIEW FRANCHISEES

☐ Develop your strategic plan for franchisee validation.
☐ Complete franchise validation phone calls.

(Weeks 2-5)

TASK 3: FRANCHISE DISCLOSURE DOCUMENT REVIEW

☐ Carefully review the Franchise Disclosure Documents.
☐ Review the documents with your franchise development representatives.

(Weeks 2-4)

TASK 5: BUILD ACCURATE CASH-FLOW PROJECTIONS

☐ Build cash-flow projections based on franchisee interviews.
☐ Email cash flows to target franchisees and make follow-up calls to review your projections.

(Weeks 3-5)

TASK 6: FINALIZE FINANCING

☐ Obtain financing commitment, if needed.

(Weeks 4-6)

TASK 8: MAKE A DECISION

☐ Sign a franchise agreement or move on.

(Week 6)

TASK 7: DISCOVERY DAY

☐ Visit franchisor headquarters.

(Week 5)

GET ORGANIZED

Here are the tasks laid out for week one. Keep focused, and track this information for each franchise option under consideration.

EXERCISE 9.2: SET UP A NOTEBOOK FOR EACH FRANCHISE

FRANCHISE	DATE COMPLETED

EXERCISE 9.3: REVIEW FRANCHISE WEBSITES

FRANCHISE WEBSITE	IMPRESSION OF WEBSITE	DATE COMPLETED

EXERCISE 9.4: ESTABLISH POINT-OF-CONTACT WITH EACH FRANCHISE

Initiate contact via internet requests and follow-up phone calls.

FRANCHISE	CONTACT NAME	CONTACT PHONE #	CONTACT EMAIL	DATE COMPLETED

EXERCISE 9.5 REQUEST AND REVIEW INITIAL PACKAGES

FRANCHISE	FRANCHISE PACKAGE REQUESTED	FRANCHISE PACKAGE RECEIVED AND REVIEWED	IMPRESSION OF INITIAL PACKAGE

EXERCISE 9.6: COMPLETE THE INITIAL OVERVIEW PHONE CALLS

FRANCHISE	INITIAL OVERVIEW PHONE CALL SCHEDULED	INITIAL OVERVIEW PHONE COMPLETED

On the first call, the franchisor will normally do most of the talking. In most cases they have a standard presentation that will give you a good foundational introduction to their opportunity. By the end of this call you should have a basic understanding of the:

✔ business model and

✔ product or service (from the consumer perspective).

If there are information gaps, ask follow-up questions until you are sure you have your arms around these basics. In addition, here are suggested questions for your first call.

Q: **How many franchisees do you currently have signed? How many stores are open and operating?**

A: _____

Q: **How many people are in your support staff at your corporate headquarters (not including the franchise development team)?**

A: _____

Q: **What is the future of the industry? Can you share any industry insights?**

A: _____

_____

_____

Q: **What competitive advantages does your brand have over your competition?**

A: _____

_____

_____

Q: **What skill sets are needed to be a top owner within your franchise system?**

A: _____

_____

_____

Q: **What are the traits and strengths of your most successful franchisees?**

A: _____

_____

_____

Q: **What is your standard process for helping me to learn about your franchise?**

A: _____

_____

_____

You need to begin to position yourself as an ideal candidate for their business (as well as find your own comfort level that you truly are an ideal candidate). The franchisor may begin their screening process on this first call. Be prepared to answer the following questions.

Q: **Why are you exploring entrepreneurship?**

A: _____

_____

_____

Q: **Why do you think you will be a good business owner?**

A: _____

_____

_____

Q: **What attracted you to seek more information about our franchise?**

A: _____

_____

_____

Q: **What is your timeframe for making a decision (see page 72)?**

A: _____

LOOK OUT FOR TWO-WAY STREETS

It is with great clarity that you know what you seek and what you need. But did you know that strong franchisors are as selective about who they partner with as you are? Are you a good fit for the franchisor? Strong franchisors seek candidates that have strong work ethic, personal drive, people skills, system orientation, decisiveness, and a positive attitude.

How close are you to the ideal franchise candidate? If any of the above-mentioned characteristics are areas of weakness, you need to be extremely cautious about moving forward. If you cannot foster these characteristics in yourself, then you probably should not consider franchising. If these are areas of strength, no matter the industry, you will be attractive to franchisors.

 ### A WORD TO THE WISE

As you begin conversations with the franchisors, think about how you will position yourself as the ideal candidate. You cannot turn down an opportunity that is not offered to you. Remember, this is a process of mutual evaluation. Make sure the franchisor is truly selective in how they identify good partners and make sure the franchisor wants to offer you a franchise.

REVIEW FRANCHISE DISCLOSURE DOCUMENTS

The Franchise Disclosure Document (FDD) is a very important tool for learning about a franchise system. The primary objective of due diligence is to gain a balanced picture of the franchise opportunity. The FDD is a document that you can rely on to provide information in a straightforward, transparent, and predictable format. Refer to chapter 7 of *The Educated Franchisee* for tips, advice, and red flags when reviewing documents.

As always, organization is critical. Reviewing the FDD is no exception. After initiating contact with the franchisors and completing initial overview calls, ask them to email and/or send you a copy of their FDD. The law currently states that the franchisor must provide a copy of the FDD "upon reasonable request." If you prove yourself to be a viable candidate, the franchisor must give you the FDD. If the franchisor will not release this document until you meet them face-to-face, find another franchise.

These days many franchisors are providing the FDD in an electronic format. You are able to download the document in a PDF file to your computer. While this is much faster, we suggest that you visit your local copy center and print the entire FDD on three-hole paper and put the FDD in a binder, or ask the franchisor to mail you a hard copy of this document. While reading the FDD, it is critical that you have a place to highlight wording that is unclear as well as write in notes and questions. Having the FDD in a printed format allows you to be more organized and efficient.

Once you receive the FDD, you will be required to sign the "Receipt" (item 23) and return it to the franchisor. This way the franchisor has record of the disclosure and the associated date. Signing this Receipt does not obligate you. It is simply a record of the disclosure; therefore, it should be completed in a timely fashion.

EXERCISE 9.7: TRACKING KEY DATES OF FDD REVIEW

Below you can track key FDD dates.

	FRANCHISE A: _____	FRANCHISE B: _____	FRANCHISE C: _____
Initial Overview Call Completed			
Date FDD Requested			
Date FDD Received			
Date FDD Receipt Returned			
Date of Initial FDD Review Completed			

✎ EXERCISE 9.8: COLLECTING KEY FDD DATA

As you review each item in the Franchise Disclosure Documents, use the charts below to track your questions, concerns, and overall impressions. Please duplicate these charts for each franchise you are reviewing (for additional copies, go to the download section of http://educatedfranchisee.com).

Item 1: The Franchisor and its Parents, Predecessors and Affiliates

FRANCHISE NAME:	
Summary	
Questions	
Concerns	
Overall Impression	

Item 2: Business Experience

FRANCHISE NAME:	
Summary	
Questions	
Concerns	
Overall Impression	

Item 3: Litigation

FRANCHISE NAME:	
Summary	
Questions	
Concerns	
Overall Impression	

Item 4: Bankruptcy

FRANCHISE NAME:	
Summary	
Questions	
Concerns	
Overall Impression	

Item 5: Franchise Fees

FRANCHISE NAME:	
Summary	
Questions	
Concerns	
Overall Impression	

Item 6: Other Fees

FRANCHISE NAME:	
Summary	
Questions	
Concerns	
Overall Impression	

Item 7: Estimated Initial Investment

FRANCHISE NAME:	
Summary	
Questions	
Concerns	
Overall Impression	

Item 8: Restrictions on Sources of Products and Services

FRANCHISE NAME:	
Summary	
Questions	
Concerns	
Overall Impression	

Item 9: Franchisee's Obligations

FRANCHISE NAME:	
Summary	
Questions	
Concerns	
Overall Impression	

Item 10: Financing

FRANCHISE NAME:	
Summary	
Questions	
Concerns	
Overall Impression	

Item 11: Franchisor's Assistance with Advertising, Computer Systems and Training

FRANCHISE NAME:	
Summary	
Questions	
Concerns	
Overall Impression	

Item 12: Territory

FRANCHISE NAME:	
Summary	
Questions	
Concerns	
Overall Impression	

Item 13: Trademarks

FRANCHISE NAME:	
Summary	
Questions	
Concerns	
Overall Impression	

Item 14: Patents, Copyrights and Proprietary Information

FRANCHISE NAME:	
Summary	
Questions	
Concerns	
Overall Impression	

Item 15: Obligation to Participate in the Actual Operation of the Franchise

FRANCHISE NAME:	
Summary	
Questions	
Concerns	
Overall Impression	

Item 16: Restrictions on What the Franchisee May Sell

FRANCHISE NAME:	
Summary	
Questions	
Concerns	
Overall Impression	

Item 17: Renewal, Termination, Transfer and Dispute Resolution

FRANCHISE NAME:	
Summary	
Questions	
Concerns	
Overall Impression	

Item 18: Arrangements with Public Figures

FRANCHISE NAME:	
Summary	
Questions	
Concerns	
Overall Impression	

Item 19: Financial Performance Representations

FRANCHISE NAME:	
Summary	
Questions	
Concerns	
Overall Impression	

Item 20: Outlets and Franchisee Information

FRANCHISE NAME:	
Summary	
Questions	
Concerns	
Overall Impression	

Item 21: Financial Statements

FRANCHISE NAME:	
Summary	
Questions	
Concerns	
Overall Impression	

Item 22: Contracts

FRANCHISE NAME:	
Summary	
Questions	
Concerns	
Overall Impression	

Item 23: Receipt

FRANCHISE NAME:	
Date Received	
Date Receipt Returned	

NOTES

_____

_____

_____

_____

_____

_____

_____

_____

_____

_____

_____

EXERCISE 9.9: COMPARE KEY FDD DATA

Below is a chart to track key comparison data found in the FDDs.

	ITEM #	FRANCHISE A: _____	FRANCHISE B: _____	FRANCHISE C: _____
Year Founded	Item #1			
Year Franchising Began	Item #1			
Experience Level of the Franchisor in Their Industry	Item #2			
Experience Level of the Franchisor in Franchising	Item #2			
Number/Manner of Lawsuits	Item #3			
History of Bankruptcy	Item #4			

Franchise Fee	Item #5			
Royalty	Item #6			
Advertising Fee (national, local, co-op)	Item #6			
Other Fees	Item #6			
Estimated Initial Investment (low to high)	Item #7			
Does the Franchisor offer any In-house Financing	Item #10			
Summary of Initial Training	Item #11			

Territory Protections	Item #12			
Full-time Work Requirement	Item #15			
How Long is the Term of Agreement	Item #17			
Financial Performance Representation	Item #19			
Number of Franchisees • Last year • Two years ago • Three years ago	Item #20			
Success Rate in a 3-year Period	Item #20			
Financial Strength of Franchisor	Item #21			

Franchise Disclosure Document review is a critical task when it comes to understanding a franchise business opportunity. A thorough review of the FDD will allow you to go into a business with your eyes wide open.

The FDD is designed to help you identify red flags or reasons not to move forward with a franchise system. It does very little to help you understand why a franchise is successful or how it will compete in the marketplace. Fortunately, the next step will help you better understand the strengths of the franchise system. Talking with franchisees is where the business comes alive. You will truly begin to understand the day-to-day life of a franchisee and the real income potential. By reviewing the FDD and then speaking with franchisees, you will gain a well-rounded, balanced view of the franchise.

"I promise . . . to remember this is a mutual evaluation process. Unless an obvious roadblock occurs, such as lack of territory, I will remain focused. I will carefully review and fully understand the Franchise Disclosure Documents. I will work through anxiety to gain knowledge and understanding."

X _____   X _____

                 Signature   **Date**

Step 10: The Art of the Interview

"The quality of your life equals the quality of the questions you ask yourself."

~ Tony Robbins (born February 29, 1960)
American self-help writer and professional speaker

PURPOSE

» **Target franchisees for validation.**

» **Compile thoughtful, pertinent questions for the franchisees.**

» **Complete focused validation calls.**

» **Capture key impressions from validation.**

Mother knows best? Father knows best? Your accountant knows best? Your lawyer knows best? Your development rep knows best? Your cousin's best friend's step-dad knows best? Who is it? Who can give you the BEST insight on any franchise?

If you were to apply for a new job and had access to anyone and everyone to help you understand the job so you could make a really smart decision, who would you want to talk to? Would you turn to your mother, your father, your accountant, your lawyer, the interviewer? They will certainly all have strong opinions, but they also could unintentionally give you really bad advice.

When you interview for a job, the employer rarely gives you the name and phone numbers of all the folks who hold or have held this position in the past three years so you can call them "off line" and "chat." But with franchising, it is mandated that the franchisors provide you with the name, address, and contact information for franchisees that have gone before you. The current and past franchisees are your best resource. THIS is where true insights are gained—from the folks who have been in or are in the trenches!

For the sake of clarity and manageability, the validation calls are separated into two steps. This first step reveals a "day in the life" of a franchisee, including how to gather information on training, systems, support, and much more. The next step focuses on how to gain a clear and accurate understanding of the return potential.

It is natural for you to want to call franchisees that are next door to your target market area. The closest franchisees seem like they could be most helpful, but be VERY careful. The reason you call franchisees is to gain unbiased information. Your entry into the marketplace may have an impact on the franchisee located down the road from you. As a result, their comments may be biased. They may give you the straight scoop, or they may try to scare you off of what they perceive to be their future growth area.

Additionally, they may try to buy the territory from the franchisor before you do. It is not uncommon for a prospective franchisee to lose an opportunity due to an existing neighboring franchisee purchasing the territory. Wait to make these calls until the end of your investigation, and enter the conversations with your eyes wide open.

TARGET FRANCHISEES

First you should gather your list of target franchisees. With the help of the franchisor, ask for suggestions as to which owners to call (focus on those who are the best owners in the franchise system). Review chapter 11 of *The Educated Franchisee* for a full description of each type of franchisee you should contact and why. Don't call yet! Just get your targets and questions organized. Note that there are specific questions to ask each target group.

NOTES

_____

_____

_____

_____

_____

_____

_____

_____

_____

_____

_____

✎ EXERCISE 10.1: THE BEST

First target the best owners. If the top owners are not happy or do not meet your expectations, there is no reason to continue.

FRANCHISE A: _____

	FRANCHISEE NAME	LOCATION	PHONE NUMBER
1			
2			

FRANCHISE B: _____

	FRANCHISEE NAME	LOCATION	PHONE NUMBER
1			
2			

FRANCHISE C: _____

	FRANCHISEE NAME	LOCATION	PHONE NUMBER
1			
2			

✎ EXERCISE 10.2: NEW FRANCHISEES

It is important to call a few new franchisees—folks who have been franchisees for three to nine months. These franchisees can help you better understand the current training and start-up support. Ask the franchisor or other owners to help you identify these targets.

FRANCHISE A: _____

	FRANCHISEE NAME	LOCATION	PHONE NUMBER
1			
2			

FRANCHISE B: _____

	FRANCHISEE NAME	LOCATION	PHONE NUMBER
1			
2			

FRANCHISE C: _____

	FRANCHISEE NAME	LOCATION	PHONE NUMBER
1			
2			

✎ EXERCISE 10.3: FRANCHISEES WITH LIKE BACKGROUNDS

The normal franchise system is filled with people from many different backgrounds. Each individual has different life experiences and different expectations. If you can speak with franchisees that are similar to you in regard to skills, expectations, and/or life experiences, you will gain invaluable insights. These individuals may see the world from your same shoes and be able give you insights that others may not.

FRANCHISE A: _____

	FRANCHISEE NAME	LOCATION	PHONE NUMBER
1			
2			

FRANCHISE B: _____

	FRANCHISEE NAME	LOCATION	PHONE NUMBER
1			
2			

FRANCHISE C: _____

	FRANCHISEE NAME	LOCATION	PHONE NUMBER
1			
2			

EXERCISE 10.4: FRANCHISEES THAT ARE SELLING, CLOSING OR HAVE LEFT THE SYSTEM

It is fair to ask a franchisor for the name of franchisees that have their businesses for sale or have closed their franchise. Finding out why a person is selling or has closed can give you valuable insights in regard to how to increase your potential for success.

FRANCHISE A: _____

	FRANCHISEE NAME	LOCATION	PHONE NUMBER
1			
2			

FRANCHISE B: _____

	FRANCHISEE NAME	LOCATION	PHONE NUMBER
1			
2			

FRANCHISE C: _____

	FRANCHISEE NAME	LOCATION	PHONE NUMBER
1			
2			

✎ EXERCISE 10.5: RANDOM CALLS TO FRANCHISEES

After you have identified your target franchisees, select a group of random franchisees to call. Use the list in the Franchise Disclosure Document to pick your target list of random owners. Where possible, look for franchisees in markets similar to yours.

FRANCHISE A: _____

	FRANCHISEE NAME	LOCATION	PHONE NUMBER
1			
2			

Franchise B: _____

	FRANCHISEE NAME	LOCATION	PHONE NUMBER
1			
2			

FRANCHISE C: _____

	FRANCHISEE NAME	LOCATION	PHONE NUMBER
1			
2			

CALL FRANCHISEES

Now that you have your list of target franchisees, it is time to pick up the phone. Never underestimate or shorten this step. It is the cornerstone to a smart, informed decision. Busy franchisees may be tough to reach, so be persistent. Do not expect them to call you back. Always remember, the more they like you the more time they will take with you and the more insights they will provide. A suggested starter list of questions to ask franchisees follows.

✏ EXERCISE 10.6: QUESTIONS TO ASK FRANCHISEES

Review all of the questions below and customize the list for each franchise system. This will allow you to get organized before you pick up the phone. You may not have time to ask every question of every franchisee, so use your time wisely.

HISTORY AND COMPETENCY

- ☐ How long have you been a franchisee?
- ☐ What was your professional background/previous career?
- ☐ Why did you leave that?

COMPETITIVENESS

- ☐ What advantages and disadvantages does this franchise have over its competitors?
- ☐ What is the most valuable part of the franchise system in helping you to effectively compete?

EXPECTATIONS

- ☐ What is your hourly commitment per week? How has this changed over time?
- ☐ Did your due diligence properly prepare you for the business? If not, what surprised you?

GOAL ACHIEVEMENT

- ☐ Why did you invest in this franchise?
- ☐ Would you invest in this franchise all over again? Why/why not? If not, are you selling?

LEADERSHIP VALIDATION

- ☐ Is the home office competent?
- ☐ Does the home office act with your best interests in mind? Can you give an example?

MARKETING

- [ ] How does the franchisor contribute to your marketing efforts? What would you change?
- [ ] Is the franchise company's advertising program effective?
- [ ] What additional things do you do to generate business?

PERFORMANCE

- [ ] What's the biggest mistake that first-year franchisees make?
- [ ] What's the smartest thing a first-year franchisee can do?
- [ ] What would cause a franchisee to fail?

RELATIONSHIPS

- [ ] Does the franchisor honestly care about your results/success? Can you give an example?
- [ ] Do you feel you have a positive rapport with the franchisor and your fellow franchisees?
- [ ] What do you like most/least about your franchise relationship?

SUPPORT

- [ ] Does the franchisor support your business activities and results to the level of your expectations?
- [ ] Does the franchisor respond promptly to your concerns?
- [ ] How could the franchisor improve ongoing support?

A DAY IN THE LIFE OF AN OWNER

- [ ] Tell me about a typical day.
- [ ] How have your responsibilities changed over time?
- [ ] What are the most important tasks to ensure the business is successful?

SYSTEMS

- [ ] What are the advantages of being with this franchise versus being on your own? Disadvantages?
- [ ] Could you have done this as effectively on your own?
- [ ] Why did you choose this franchise?

SPECIFIC QUESTIONS FOR THE BEST OWNERS WITHIN THE FRANCHISE

- ☐ What separates high-performing franchisees from low-performing franchisees?
- ☐ What do you attribute your success to with this franchise?
- ☐ What are the most important tasks you do each day to reach your goals?

SPECIFIC QUESTIONS FOR OWNERS IN BUSINESS ONE YEAR OR LESS

- ☐ Did your initial training prepare you for opening and operating this business?
- ☐ How could the franchisor improve initial training?
- ☐ Have the initial support programs been sufficient?
- ☐ Can you define any difference between your initial investment and the total investment of $_____ as described in Item 7 of the FDD? (Before you ask this question, look up the total investment in Item 7 of each company FDD)
- ☐ Is there anything you know now that you wish you knew when you started this business?

SPECIFIC QUESTIONS FOR OWNERS WITH LIKE BACKGROUNDS

- ☐ Has your experience/background been an advantage or disadvantage in starting your business?
- ☐ What is your least favorite part of the business?
- ☐ What is your favorite part of the business?

SPECIFIC QUESTIONS FOR FRANCHISEES THAT ARE SELLING, CLOSING OR HAVE LEFT THE SYSTEM

- ☐ How long were you operating your franchise?
- ☐ Did you sell your business, or close your doors?
- ☐ If you closed your doors, why did you do this?
- ☐ If you sold your business, did you sell your business for a profit or loss? What percentage of one year's net did the business sell for? What was the sale price?

SUMMARIZE KEY IMPRESSIONS

You have now spoken with a large number of franchisees and have gathered a lot of information. Much of the information is very detailed. Don't get lost in the weeds! Often, folks are so worried about the details (such as the efficacy rate of the direct mail program that happens in the third month) that they forget to measure their overall comfort with the concept and the franchisees. Take a minute to capture your key impressions from your conversations.

✏ EXERCISE 10.7: KEY IMPRESSIONS FROM THE FRANCHISEES

FRANCHISE A: _____

What are the main strengths and challenges of this franchise?

_____

_____

_____

Is the franchisor doing a good job with support and systems? Are the owners happy?

_____

_____

_____

Do I share in the strengths, skill sets, and work ethic of top owners?

_____

_____

_____

Would I enjoy the daily tasks to make this business a success?

_____

_____

_____

Do I feel comfortable with the franchisee community and do I feel that I would fit in?

_____

_____

_____

Can I visualize myself operating a successful business in this franchise system?

_____

_____

_____

FRANCHISE B: _____

What are the main strengths and challenges of this franchise?

_____

_____

_____

Is the franchisor doing a good job with support and systems? Are the owners happy?

_____

_____

_____

Do I share in the strengths, skill sets, and work ethic of top owners?

_____

_____

_____

Would I enjoy the daily tasks to make this business a success?

_____

_____

_____

Do I feel comfortable with the franchisee community and do I feel that I would fit in?

_____

_____

_____

Can I visualize myself operating a successful business in this franchise system?

_____

_____

_____

Franchise C: _____

What are the main strengths and challenges of this franchise?

_____

_____

_____

Is the franchisor doing a good job with support and systems? Are the owners happy?

_____

_____

_____

Do I share in the strengths, skill sets, and work ethic of top owners?

_____

_____

_____

Would I enjoy the daily tasks to make this business a success?

_____

_____

_____

Do I feel comfortable with the franchisee community and do I feel that I would fit in?

_____

_____

_____

Can I visualize myself operating a successful business in this franchise system?

_____

_____

_____

🦉 A WORD TO THE WISE

As you look back on all the calls you made, did you feel more comfortable with one group of franchisees? If so, this is a good sign. It is important that you feel at home with your fellow franchisees.

"**I promise** . . . to be persistent and thorough in owner validation calls. I will continue to make calls until I am confident I have a realistic understanding of the: business model, competitive advantages, support systems, and typical day in the life of the franchisee."

X _____   X _____

Signature   **Date**

🍎 NOTES

_____

_____

_____

_____

_____

_____

_____

_____

_____

_____

_____

_____

_____

Step 11: Learn the Science of Numbers

"Financial literacy is not an end in itself, but a step-by-step process."

~ Carl R. George
Chairman of the National CPA
Financial Literacy Commission

PURPOSE

» Understand the value of a top-down research method and cash-flow projections.

» Follow these six key steps to create accurate cash-flow projections utilizing the knowledge and experience of current franchisees.

As you talk with franchisees, the potential of franchise ownership becomes more real. Is your mind starting to race? Take a deep breath. Finally, the step you have been eager to get to. It is time to put together cash-flow projections. As Robert Kiyosaki, author of the *Rich Dad, Poor Dad* series, aptly states: "If you want to be successful on the right side when it comes to money, you have got to know the difference between facts and opinions. You must know numbers. You must know the facts." This step will explain the most efficient way to get the facts and build accurate cash-flow projections.

TOP-DOWN RESEARCH METHOD AND CASH-FLOW PROJECTIONS

In this step, the top-down research method, as described in chapter 12 of *The Educated Franchisee*, will be used. If you have not read this chapter or do not remember the contents, read it again. Take a look at the following simplified cash-flow projections. The spreadsheets may seem intimidating, but in the end they are really very simple. In its simplest form, a cash-flow projection is income minus expenses. At the top is the income—how much money the business brings in; next comes all of the expenses—the money the business pays out; what is left is the net profit or owner benefit.

SAMPLE CASH-FLOW PROJECTION FOR A SERVICE BUSINESS

	Month 1	Month 2	Month 3	Month 4	Month 5	Month 6	Month 7	Month 8	Month 9	Month 10	Month 11	Month 12
Revenue												
Sales	$5,000	$8,000	$11,000	$14,000	$17,000	$20,000	$23,000	$26,000	$29,000	$32,000	$35,000	$38,000
Operating Expenses												
Cost of Labor	$1,500	$2,400	$3,300	$4,200	$5,100	$6,000	$6,900	$7,800	$8,700	$9,600	$10,500	$11,400
Cost of Materials	$700	$1,000	$1,300	$1,600	$1,900	$2,200	$2,500	$2,800	$3,100	$3,400	$3,700	$4,000
Office Space	$1,500	$1,500	$1,500	$1,500	$1,500	$1,500	$1,500	$1,500	$1,500	$1,500	$1,500	$1,500
Utilities	$200	$200	$200	$200	$200	$200	$200	$200	$200	$200	$200	$200
Marketing	$4,000	$4,000	$4,000	$4,000	$4,000	$4,000	$4,000	$4,000	$4,000	$4,000	$4,000	$4,000
Maintenance	$400	$400	$400	$400	$400	$400	$400	$400	$400	$400	$400	$400
Auto/Truck Lease	$575	$575	$575	$575	$575	$575	$575	$575	$575	$575	$575	$575
Auto/Truck Insurance	$300	$300	$300	$300	$300	$300	$300	$300	$300	$300	$300	$300
Auto/Truck Fuel	$70	$100	$130	$160	$190	$220	$250	$280	$310	$340	$370	$400
Communication	$150	$150	$150	$150	$150	$150	$150	$150	$150	$150	$150	$150
Royalty	$450	$720	$990	$1,260	$1,530	$1,800	$2,070	$2,340	$2,610	$2,880	$3,150	$3,420
Professional Fees	$200	$200	$200	$200	$200	$200	$200	$200	$200	$200	$200	$200
Postage & Shipping	$50	$50	$50	$50	$50	$50	$50	$50	$50	$50	$50	$50
Office Supplies	$100	$100	$100	$100	$100	$100	$100	$100	$100	$100	$100	$100
Entertainment	$300	$300	$300	$300	$300	$300	$300	$300	$300	$300	$300	$300
Additional Insurance	$200	$200	$200	$200	$200	$200	$200	$200	$200	$200	$200	$200
Miscellaneous	$500	$500	$500	$500	$500	$500	$500	$500	$500	$500	$500	$500
Total Expenses	$11,195	$12,695	$14,195	$15,695	$17,195	$18,695	$20,195	$21,695	$23,195	$24,695	$26,195	$27,695
Net Profit	$(6,195)	$(4,695)	$(3,195)	$(1,695)	$(195)	$1,305	$2,805	$4,305	$5,805	$7,305	$8,805	$10,305

This cash-flow projection is not intended to represent any particular franchise and is designed for demonstration purposes only.

STEP 11 | LEARN THE SCIENCE OF NUMBERS

SAMPLE CASH-FLOW PROJECTION FOR A RETAIL BUSINESS

	Month 1	Month 2	Month 3	Month 4	Month 5	Month 6	Month 7	Month 8	Month 9	Month 10	Month 11	Month 12
Revenue												
Sales	$10,000	$15,000	$20,000	$25,000	$30,000	$35,000	$40,000	$45,000	$50,000	$55,000	$60,000	$65,000
Cost of Goods Sold	$4,000	$6,000	$8,000	$10,000	$12,000	$14,000	$16,000	$18,000	$20,000	$22,000	$24,000	$26,000
Gross Profit	$6,000	$9,000	$12,000	$15,000	$18,000	$21,000	$24,000	$27,000	$30,000	$33,000	$36,000	$39,000
Operating Expenses												
Cost of Labor	$6,000	$6,000	$6,000	$6,000	$7,000	$7,500	$8,000	$8,000	$10,000	$10,000	$10,000	$10,000
Lease Expense	$4,000	$4,000	$4,000	$4,000	$4,000	$4,000	$4,000	$4,000	$4,000	$4,000	$4,000	$4,000
Utilities	$500	$500	$500	$500	$500	$500	$500	$500	$500	$500	$500	$500
Marketing	$4,000	$4,000	$4,000	$4,000	$4,000	$4,000	$4,000	$4,000	$4,000	$4,000	$4,000	$4,000
Maintenance	$400	$400	$400	$400	$400	$400	$400	$400	$400	$400	$400	$400
Communication	$300	$300	$300	$300	$300	$300	$300	$300	$300	$300	$300	$300
Royalty	$700	$1,050	$1,400	$1,750	$2,100	$2,450	$2,800	$3,150	$3,500	$3,850	$4,200	$4,550
Supplies	$300	$300	$300	$300	$300	$300	$300	$300	$300	$300	$300	$300
Entertainment	$300	$300	$300	$300	$300	$300	$300	$300	$300	$300	$300	$300
Professional Fees	$250	$250	$250	$250	$250	$250	$250	$250	$250	$250	$250	$250
Insurance	$200	$200	$200	$200	$200	$200	$200	$200	$200	$200	$200	$200
Miscellaneous	$500	$500	$500	$500	$500	$500	$500	$500	$500	$500	$500	$500
Total Expenses	$17,450	$17,800	$18,150	$18,500	$19,850	$20,700	$21,550	$21,900	$24,250	$24,600	$24,950	$25,300
Net Profit	$(11,450)	$(8,800)	$(6,150)	$(3,500)	$(1,850)	$300	$2,450	$5,100	$5,750	$8,400	$11,050	$13,700

This cash-flow projection is not intended to represent any particular franchise and is designed for demonstration purposes only.

6 STEPS TO BUILD ACCURATE FINANCIAL PROJECTIONS

The goal of this section is to make sure you fully understand all of the income and expense line items for your target franchises in order to build accurate financial projections. Follow these steps to create your own cash-flow projections.

EXERCISE 11.1: LIST INCOME AND EXPENSE ITEMS

Make a list of all income and expense line items for each company. The list does not have to be perfect. Just do your best. You may even want to ask the franchisor development representative if they can help you in this area. Many will be happy to give you the income and expense line items.

Sample Income Line Items:

- Product
- Service
- Other

Sample Expenses Line Items:

- Labor
- Cost of Materials
- Rent
- Communication
- Supplies
- Royalty
- Vehicles
- Marketing
- Insurance
- Maintenance
- Entertainment
- Other

What other expenses do you think would apply to Franchise A, B, and C?

FRANCHISE A: _____

_____

FRANCHISE B: _____

_____

FRANCHISE C: _____

_____

EXERCISE 11.2: CREATE A SPREADSHEET

Transfer income/expense data into a spreadsheet format. Then begin to add the details. If the FDD provides income and expense information in Item 19, transfer this information to the spreadsheet. If you have been on conference calls that provided some guidance, include that information. Or, if you already have knowledge of how the income and expenses should work, add this information. Do your best based on the information you have. Do not stress if you are unsure of your estimates and do not allow this step to take more than one hour of your time for each option. Just get some numbers down on paper or in Excel format. You will verify and correct everything shortly.

SAMPLE BLANK CASH-FLOW PROJECTION

	Month 1	Month 2	Month 3	Month 4	Month 5	Month 6	Month 7	Month 8	Month 9	Month 10	Month 11	Month 12
Revenue												
Operating Expenses												
Total Expenses												
Net Profit												

Most people will want to expand their analysis beyond twelve months. It is most common to gather estimates for three years into the future. Some people also run pessimistic, realistic, and optimistic spreadsheets to show the ranges and averages found within a franchise system.

✎ EXERCISE 11.3: IDENTIFY TARGET FRANCHISEES

Identify franchisees you would like to have review your cash flows. Think of owners who you had a strong rapport with during the last step of general validation. You can also ask the franchise development representatives for help to identify owners who are willing and able to review spreadsheets. Some franchisees are exceptionally competent in this area and enjoy helping. They can be of great assistance.

FRANCHISE A: _____

OWNER NAME	OWNER PHONE NUMBER	OWNER EMAIL ADDRESS

FRANCHISE B: _____

OWNER NAME	OWNER PHONE NUMBER	OWNER EMAIL ADDRESS

FRANCHISE C: _____

OWNER NAME	OWNER PHONE NUMBER	OWNER EMAIL ADDRESS

EXERCISE 11.4: CONTACT TARGET FRANCHISEES

Call your target franchisees and ask if they could help you better understand the income and expense side of the business. Owners might be offended if you ask them how much money they make, but few can resist the invitation to show what they know. First confirm that you have all of the income and expense line items. Then, review each line item individually in order to make sure you fully understand each line item.

For example, one expense line item might be marketing. You might ask, how much do you spend on marketing each month? Do you spend the same amount on marketing each month or do you vary the amount based on the season? How did you decide to spend this much each month? Use the information to fine-tune your projections.

Do this for each expense and you will have a strong understanding of how each expense works. Repeat this step with other franchisees until you are confident you have a realistic understanding of the return potential. With each review, you will be closer and closer to selecting a franchise that best fits your needs and goals.

Once you have fine-tuned your projections and you believe you have a fair understanding of all the income and expenses, then you can move on to exercise 11.5.

EXERCISE 11.5: SHARE FINAL PROJECTIONS WITH TARGET FRANCHISEES

Email your final projections to a few select franchisees. Ask if they will review your projections to determine if you have misunderstood anything. Then, set up a phone call to review your spreadsheets. This final step will ensure you have accurate projections.

"It is better by noble boldness to run the risk of being subject to half the evils we anticipate than to remain in cowardly listlessness for fear of what might happen."

—Herodotus (485–425 BC), Greek historian

EXERCISE 11.6: ESTIMATE OWNER BENEFIT

Estimate owner benefit. Profitability will, of course, vary owner by owner. But each franchise system does have ranges and averages. You should work to get a feel for the range and the averages. Summarize your impressions of average owner benefit here.

ESTIMATED AVERAGE OWNER BENEFIT

	YEAR ONE	YEAR TWO	YEAR THREE	TOP OWNERS
Franchise A: _____				
Franchise B: _____				
Franchise C: _____				

Return to page 59 to review your net income goals. How close does each franchise get to your objective? As you understand the return potential of your target options, you will be able to determine if each franchise is a viable alternative to traditional employment. When you review this information, remember cash flow is only one of the attractive aspects of a franchise. You must not overlook the asset value of the business as it grows, as well as the tax benefits and lifestyle advantages a business can provide.

> **"I promise . . .** I will not assume the profitability of a franchise. I will utilize franchisees to the fullest to ensure I have a realistic understanding of average return and profitability of a franchise."
>
> X _____ X _____
>
> **Signature**   **Date**

Step 12: Identify the Best Loan Options

PURPOSE

» **Explore national, franchisor-preferred, and local loan options.**

» **Track and compare finance options.**

» **Select the best option based on facts and terms.**

In some ways, buying a franchise is analogous to purchasing a home. You walk into the house and see a shiny new kitchen and gleaming pool. The real estate agent approaches and starts talking about schools, lot lines, roofs, etc., but all you can think of is, *Can I afford this house?* It is not until you have met with the loan officer and he or she gives you the "go ahead" that you really listen to the attributes of the home and fully consider your options.

Follow these steps to ensure you understand the widest range of finance options available to you. Do not assume you know the best option. Do the research and let the facts direct your actions.

First, reread chapter 13 of *The Educated Franchisee*. It is important that you understand the various types of funding alternatives and know the difference between debt and equity funding before you identify target lenders.

NATIONAL LENDERS

Next, complete a general search online to identify national lenders that specialize in franchise financing. Visit https://educatedfranchisee.com/resources/franchise-funding-finance for a list of reputable organizations. It makes sense to begin your search with the lenders most familiar with franchising and its benefits.

EXERCISE 12.1: NATIONAL LENDERS THAT SPECIALIZE IN FRANCHISING

List your target national lenders below.

National Lender	
Website	
Contact Name	
Telephone Number	
Email Address	

National Lender	
Website	
Contact Name	
Telephone Number	
Email Address	

National Lender	
Website	
Contact Name	
Telephone Number	
Email Address	

FRANCHISOR-PREFERRED LENDERS

The next avenue to explore is the franchisor's funding sources. Many good franchisors have established relationships with lenders that understand and respect the quality of the franchise and may be interested in funding new franchise units. Some franchisors also offer in-house financing. If in-house financing is available it will be detailed in Item 10 in the Franchise Disclosure Document.

EXERCISE 12.2: FRANCHISOR-PREFERRED LENDERS

List your target franchisor-preferred lenders below.

Preferred Lender	
Website	
Contact Name	
Telephone Number	
Email Address	

Preferred Lender	
Website	
Contact Name	
Telephone Number	
Email Address	

LOCAL BANKS

Once you understand the options offered by national lenders and you have explored preferred franchisor lenders, you may wish to make an appointment with your local bank. In reality, your local bank branch is rarely the best financing alternative since they are often unfamiliar with the intricacies of each franchise and find it difficult to evaluate these opportunities and assess risk.

✎ EXERCISE 12.3: LOCAL BANKS

List your target local lenders below.

Local Lender	
Website	
Contact Name	
Telephone Number	
Email Address	

Once your target lenders are identified, call them or visit them and give each potential lending source a copy of your net worth found on page 20 of this workbook. You should also look up and share your current credit score. This can be done online with minimal or no charge at sites such as www.annualcreditreport.com. When you order this information, be sure to request your credit "score" as well as your credit "report." If you have this information ahead of time and share it with the lenders, you will reduce the total number of credit checks and protect your credit score.

Current Credit Score: _____

As you talk with lenders, strive to understand your broadest range of loan options. You have to look at all options in order to understand which is best. Ask each lender if they can help with any or all of the following loan options, and have them explain the terms. Use the following Finance Tracking Chart to record their answers.

- ✔ HELOC (Home Equity Line of Credit)
- ✔ Equipment Loan or Equipment Leasing
- ✔ Rollover for Business Start-Up (ROBS)
- ✔ Signature Loan or Personal Line of Credit
- ✔ SBA Guaranteed Loan (Small Business Administration)
- ✔ Business Loan or Business Line of Credit
- ✔ Other Options

FINANCE TRACKING CHART

As you explore options, use the following chart to track the information you gather. You can find copies of this form at https://educatedfranchisee.com/downloads

✎ EXERCISE 12.4: FINANCE OPTIONS

Lender	
Loan Type	
Total Project Cost for Business	
Cash Injection Amount	
Loan Amount	
Type of Collateral (home, property, certificate of deposit, other)	
Value of Required Collateral	
Interest Rate	
Length of Loan	
Penalty for Pre-payment	
Monthly Payment Amount	
Total Cost to Structure Funding (set-up or origination fees)	
Annual Cost to Maintain Funding (maintenance fees)	
Estimated Timeframe from Application to Funding	
Other	
Customer Service/Responsiveness	
Years in Lending	

*All of these categories may or may not be applicable to all funding options.

Once you understand national, franchisor-preferred, and local lending options you may want to explore non-traditional loan sources, as discussed in chapter 13 of *The Educated Franchisee*. Such sources include:

- ✔ Friends and Family
- ✔ Private Equity Investors/Angel Investors
- ✔ Peer-to-Peer Lending Networks

You should discuss the details of your options with your franchise consultant, tax advisor, and/or attorney. Good consultants understand the current lending landscape and can point you toward additional options where loans are available at attractive terms.

Once you understand your options and the terms are clarified, you are in a position to select the most attractive financing option. Look for the best terms and lowest interest rates and choose the one that makes the most sense for you. If you determine that debt financing is the best alternative for you, be sure to identify your monthly debt payment and then insert this additional expense into the Cash-Flow Projection you compiled on page 111.

"I promise . . . I will not assume I understand my best loan option but will fully explore financing options and allow the facts to direct my financing decision."

X _____   X _____

           Signature   **Date**

Step 13: Logic and Intuition—Narrow Your Focus

"Many of us have heard opportunity knocking at our door, but by the time we unhooked the chain, pushed back the bolt, turned two locks, and shut off the burglar alarm—it was gone."

~ Author unknown

PURPOSE

» **Brainstorm and identify what is important in finding the best franchise match.**

» **Use your target criteria to setup and complete a decision-making matrix.**

» **Identify the best logical match.**

» **Utilize visualization exercises to direct you to the best franchise match.**

» **Identify the best intuitive match.**

With these final exercises, you will tap into both sides of your brain to make the very best decision. As detailed in *The Educated Franchisee*, there are two types of decision makers. One type of decision maker uses the left side of the brain. These individuals are predominately logical in their approach to decision making. The other type of decision maker uses the right side of the brain. These individuals are predominately intuitive in their approach to decision making. One set of exercises will be comfortable for you, and the other will challenge you. But use both to ensure that you make a balanced decision, calling upon both your logical and intuitive sides.

CALL UPON YOUR LOGIC

Imagine you are on the showroom floor in a new car dealership. You have done your homework, researched the internet, read all the reports, talked with owners, and taken test drives, but you are still unsure which car you will be happiest with. The same thing can happen when choosing the best franchise. The following step-by-step process will help you logically pick the best franchise—that one will propel you into your future.

We will show you how to create a decision-making matrix. This allows you to collect, organize, and synthesize the data, resulting in a score to help you make an informed, educated, and logical decision. This is a time when you let the facts speak for themselves.

Curious as to the outcome? Follow these steps to see which franchise makes the most logical sense for you.

5 STEPS TO CREATE A DECISION MATRIX

✎ EXERCISE 13.1: BRAINSTORM BUSINESS CRITERIA

Brainstorm all the things that are important to you in a business. Reflect upon what you have learned throughout this workbook. What is important to you? Make a master list of all the factors. There is no need to prioritize it yet, and it doesn't matter if the list is long. Just make sure all of the factors are listed, no matter how seemingly insignificant.

1. _____
2. _____
3. _____
4. _____
5. _____
6. _____
7. _____
8. _____
9. _____
10. _____
11. _____
12. _____
13. _____
14. _____
15. _____
16. _____
17. _____
18. _____

✎ EXERCISE 13.2: NARROW THE FOCUS

Narrow the master list down to a maximum of ten criteria. Many of your items can be merged into one item. Others may not have much importance. As you whittle down the list, make sure the list is reflective of your needs and desires. Do not include an item just because someone else said it should be important. Only include those items that are honestly important to you. If it is truly important to "never work on weekends again," then list it. In the end, this will be your business.

1. _____

2. _____

3. _____

4. _____

5. _____

6. _____

7. _____

8. _____

9. _____

10. _____

✎ EXERCISE 13.3: WEIGH THE SIGNIFICANCE OF YOUR CRITERIA

Weigh the significance of your criteria. Some of the criteria will be very important to you and other criteria may not be nearly as important. Weighing the importance of criteria will allow you to adjust for these differences.

Start with 100 points and then allocate the 100 points among the 10 criteria. For example, if one criterion is of average importance, it should receive 10 points. If one is twice as important as the average, give it 20 points. If it is half as important, give it 5 points. Once you are done, step back and look at your list. Make sure it correctly reflects your values and the relative importance of each criterion.

(Chart on next page.)

CRITERIA	WEIGHT
1.	
2.	
3.	
4.	
5.	
6.	
7.	
8.	
9.	
10.	
TOTAL POINTS	100

EXERCISE 13.4: SCORE FRANCHISES BASED UPON YOUR CRITERIA

Score each franchise on each criterion you have listed. Try to be as honest as possible. If you don't remember, go back to your notes. If you cannot find the information, make some more calls. You need to be able to answer each question for each company correctly and factually. Award points based on the following system:

+ 2	points is an outstanding match to the criteria
+ 1	point is a match to the criteria
0	points for a neutral ranking
- 1	point is not a match to the criteria
- 2	points is in conflict with the criteria

Once you have finished scoring each company, step back and take a look at your answers. Make sure the scores are reflective of the facts as they relate to each franchise. Also make sure the scores are comparatively accurate from franchise to franchise.

CRITERIA	WEIGHT	FRANCHISE A: _____ SCORE	FRANCHISE B: _____ SCORE	FRANCHISE C: _____ SCORE
1.				
2.				
3.				
4.				
5.				
6.				
7.				
8.				
9.				
10.				
TOTAL POINTS	100			

EXERCISE 13.5: DETERMINE TOP LOGICAL FRANCHISE MATCH

Now it is time to do the math. Simply multiply the score by the weight and then sum the totals for each franchise. Follow the chart below:

		FRANCHISE A: _____		FRANCHISE B: _____		FRANCHISE C: _____	
CRITERIA	**WEIGHT**	**SCORE**	**TOTAL**	**SCORE**	**TOTAL**	**SCORE**	**TOTAL**
1.							
2.							
3.							
4.							
5.							
6.							
7.							
8.							
9.							
10.							
TOTAL POINTS	100						

To illustrate the exercise, here is a completed decision matrix. This example is not intended to sway you one way or the other. It is simply designed to show you how the math works and what a completed decision matrix should look like.

SAMPLE DECISION MATRIX

CRITERIA	WEIGHT	FRANCHISE A: SCORE	FRANCHISE A: TOTAL	FRANCHISE B: SCORE	FRANCHISE B: TOTAL	FRANCHISE C: SCORE	FRANCHISE C: TOTAL
1. Speed of Breakeven	8	-2	-16	0	0	2	16
2. Monday–Friday	12	-1	-12	2	24	2	24
3. Predictability	15	0	0	2	30	0	0
4. Quality of Support	4	2	8	2	8	2	8
5. Resale Valuation	12	0	0	1	12	1	12
6. Investment under $150K	17	-1	-17	2	34	1	17
7. Enjoyable	5	2	10	1	5	1	5
8. Employee Management	8	0	0	-1	-8	-1	-8
9. Strong Marketing Program	5	-2	-10	-2	-10	-1	-5
10. Meets My Financial Goals	14	0	0	0	0	1	14
TOTAL POINTS	100		-37		95		83

The above approach will help you identify the franchise that makes the best sense for you from a logical, left-brained, point of view. This does not mean that you should run out and sign a franchise agreement just yet. It just means that logically, you know which franchise best fits you and is most likely to deliver the results you seek.

EXERCISE 13.6: LOGICAL DATA SUMMARY

Using the factual data above, which franchise is the best logical fit? _____

Is there a close second? If yes, which one? _____

CALL UPON YOUR INTUITION

Now that you have completed the logical approach, gather all of your work and put it away! It is not that you want to discard the information, but now you will need to take the information that is fresh in your mind and put it to use by calling upon your intuition.

Find a time and a place where you will not have any time constraints or distractions. Relax, close your eyes, and envision yourself five years down the road as an owner of Franchise A. Bring the vision to life. Think about your days. Envision a full day. Live out every detail—see it, smell it, feel it. Visualization is a powerful tool utilized by athletes, politicians, and leaders around the world. It is time to use visualization to direct your future.

EXERCISE 13.7: INTUITION REVIEW

With the vision of your future firm in your mind, ask yourself these questions and jot down your initial gut response:

FRANCHISE A: _____

How am I spending my day?

_____

_____

_____

_____

Am I enjoying what I am doing?

_____

_____

_____

Who is around me?

_____

_____

_____

_____

_____

Am I happy?

_____

_____

_____

_____

_____

Have I created a life based on what is important to me?

_____

_____

_____

_____

How much freedom and control am I experiencing?

_____

_____

_____

_____

_____

How successful am I?

_____

_____

_____

_____

Am I financially comfortable?

_____

_____

_____

_____

How close am I to reaching my vision?

_____

_____

_____

_____

As you answer these questions and visualize your future with Franchise A, how is your body responding? Pay attention to your physiological responses. Are you stressed? Are you relaxed? Are you energized? Summarize your responses here:

_____

_____

_____

_____

_____

NOW GO THROUGH THE SAME EXERCISE WITH **FRANCHISE B.**

FRANCHISE B: _____

How am I spending my day?

_____

_____

_____

_____

Am I enjoying what I am doing?

_____

_____

_____

_____

_____

Who is around me?

_____

_____

_____

_____

_____

Am I happy?

_____

_____

_____

_____

_____

Have I created a life based on what is important to me?

_____

_____

_____

_____

How much freedom and control am I experiencing?

_____

_____

_____

_____

How successful am I?

_____

_____

_____

_____

Am I financially comfortable?

_____

_____

_____

_____

How close am I to reaching my vision?

_____

_____

_____

_____

_____

As you answer these questions and visualize your future with Franchise B, how is your body responding? Pay attention to your physiological responses. Are you stressed? Are you relaxed? Are you energized? Summarize your responses here:

_____

_____

_____

_____

_____

_____

NOW GO THROUGH THE SAME EXERCISE WITH **FRANCHISE C.**

FRANCHISE C: _____

How am I spending my day?

_____

_____

_____

_____

Am I enjoying what I am doing?

_____

_____

_____

_____

_____

Who is around me?

_____

_____

_____

_____

_____

Am I happy?

_____

_____

_____

_____

_____

Have I created a life based on what is important to me?

_____

_____

_____

_____

How much freedom and control am I experiencing?

_____

_____

_____

_____

_____

How successful am I?

_____

_____

_____

_____

_____

Am I financially comfortable?

_____

_____

_____

_____

_____

How close am I to reaching my vision?

_____

_____

_____

_____

_____

As you answer these questions and visualize your future with Franchise C, how is your body responding? Pay attention to your physiological responses. Are you stressed? Are you relaxed? Are you energized? Summarize your responses here:

_____

_____

_____

_____

_____

_____

Intuitive decisions can be as good as or better than labored decisions. If you would like to learn more about the power of intuitive decisions, read _Blink_, by Malcolm Gladwell, or _How We Decide_, by Jonah Lehrer. They both go into detail regarding the fact that with proper preparation, you can and should trust your intuitive decision-making ability.

EXERCISE 13.8: INTUITION SUMMARY

As you visualize your options, which franchise "feels" the best to you? _____
_____

Is there a close second? If yes, which one? _____
_____

🦉 A WORD TO THE WISE

Paralysis, due to information overload, is the number one killer of entrepreneurial dreams. Tapping this intuitive approach to decision-making will help you triumph over this final challenge. One franchise will stand out. One franchise should "feel" the best.

"**I promise** . . . I will look at pure facts to help identify the ideal franchise match. I understand that I need to use the data collected and remove emotion to gain significant insights. I will also trust my gut intuition to direct me to the best franchise match."

X_____   X_____

             Signature   Date

Step 14: Pull It All Together

"Analysis of several hundred people who had accumulated fortunes well beyond the million dollar mark, disclosed the fact that every one of them had the habit of reaching decisions promptly, and of changing these decisions slowly, if and when they were changed. People who fail to accumulate money, without exception, have the habit of reaching decisions slowly, and of changing these decisions quickly and often."

~ Napoleon Hill (1883–1970)
American author of personal-success literature

PURPOSE

» **Thoroughly prepare for Discovery Day.**

» **Understand that this is a decision-making event.**

» **Make a positive impression at Discovery Day to ensure you get an invitation to join the franchise.**

The previous step assisted you in determining which franchise system is right for you. But you are not done yet. You have one more step before a final decision is made and that is to meet the franchisor at their headquarters. This is typically called Discovery Day. By following these exercises you will be able to properly prepare yourself for a successful Discovery Day.

Usually you will complete these final steps with just one franchise option. But if you do have a close second you can continue with a side-by-side analysis.

Tapping my logical and emotional sides, which franchise is best?

_____

Is there a close second? If so, which one?

_____

WHAT TO EXPECT

You should schedule a face-to-face visit or Discovery Day with your target franchisor(s). As you approach Discovery Day, you need to think of it as a decision-making event. Most people find this statement scary, but let us clarify. This DOES NOT mean you need to sign a franchise agreement on Discovery Day. As a matter of fact, many quality franchisors will want to hold a staff meeting to discuss your candidacy before deciding to offer you a franchise. What it DOES mean is that you should have every question answered by the end of Discovery Day. After Discovery Day, the only thing left to do is to decide which path to take.

Discovery Day is all about a final gut check. It should instill confidence that all you have learned is accurate. You should sense a connection with the people on the chosen franchise support team. When you leave Discovery Day, you should feel energized at the thought of joining their team. If you are not, then one of two things may be going on:

1. it is not a fit and you should move on, or

2. you were ill-prepared.

The fact that you have committed significant time and energy completing this workbook, you should be properly prepared. Complete these final steps to ensure every detail is in place.

> "Only in growth, reform and change, paradoxically enough, is true security to be found."
>
> — Anne Morrow Lindbergh (1906–2001), American aviator and author

PREPARE FOR DISCOVERY DAY

✏ EXERCISE 14.2: REVIEW NOTES

Review your notes, websites, and exercises. Do you have any final questions? If so, write them down on a separate sheet of paper so you can get them answered on Discovery Day.

Step Completed: _____

✏ EXERCISE 14.3: FINALIZE TERRITORY

Finalize your territory description to be inserted into your franchise agreement.

Step Completed: _____

Territory Definition: _____

NOTE: Prior to Discovery Day, you should request a copy of the final franchise agreement you will sign should you be approved and decide to move forward.

✏ EXERCISE 14.4: FINALIZE FINANCING

Do you understand what monies are needed and when?

Step Completed: _____

NOTE: Franchise fees are paid at the time of signing the franchise agreement. Are these funds in place? Are the additional funds in place? If not, are you doing what is necessary to make sure the money is available?

✎ EXERCISE 14.5: DEFINE TIMELINE FOR FINAL STEPS

Discovery Day: _____

Target pre-training begins: _____

Target training date at franchise headquarters: _____

Target opening date: _____

NOTE: Make sure you communicate these dates with your development coordinator to ensure you are on the same page. Do not get ahead of yourself. It is human nature to want to move to tasks required to get up-and-running. But you are paying for assistance, including start-up assistance. Take advantage of the support.

Also, it is the norm to form your legal entity after you secure the rights to operate the franchise. Typically, you (as an individual) sign the franchise agreement; and then once your legal entity is formed, the agreement is transferred to the corporate entity.

"For the past 33 years, I have looked in the mirror every morning and asked myself: 'If today were the last day of my life, would I want to do what I am about to do today?' And whenever the answer has been 'no' for too many days in a row, I know I need to change something . . .

Remembering that I'll be dead soon is the most important tool I've ever encountered to help me make the big choices in life . . . Don't let the noise of others' opinions drown out your own inner voice. And most important, have the courage to follow your heart and intuition. They somehow already know what you truly want to become. Everything else is secondary."

— Steve Jobs (born February, 1955), CEO, Apple Computer; at commencement, Stanford University, 2005

DISCOVERY DAY

Go to Discovery Day with the right mindset. It is important to know that the very best franchisors only "award" franchises; they do not "sell" them.

🦉 A WORD TO THE WISE

Buying a franchise is not like buying a car. A quality franchisor will closely evaluate your personality, experience, compatibility, financial stability, work ethic, decision-making capacity, and preparation. If you do not measure up, they will not risk awarding you a franchise. Remember, the franchisor is looking for franchise partners who are enthusiastic, positive, and comfortable following systems.

At Discovery Day, make sure any final questions or issues you have are addressed. Our hope is that you finish the day with a clear sense that these are reputable, trustworthy, and knowledgeable individuals.

Go prepared, but most importantly, enjoy the day and be yourself! If you end the day with a sense that you have found a match, verbalize your eagerness to join the franchise.

"**I promise**... I will work hard to prepare myself for an insightful Discovery Day. I will continue to move toward an informed and educated decision. I understand Discovery Day is a decision-making event. I understand that good franchises 'award' a franchise and do not 'sell' a franchise. I will present myself in the best light on this day."

X _____ X _____

          Signature   **Date**

Step 15: Release the Handbrake—Make A Decision

"Until one is committed there is hesitancy, the chance to draw back, always ineffectiveness. Concerning all acts of initiative (and creation), there is one elementary truth, the ignorance of which kills countless ideas and splendid plans: that the moment one definitely commits oneself, then Providence moves, too. Whatever you can do, or dream you can, begin it. Boldness has genius, power, and magic in it."

~ Johann Wolfgang von Goethe (1749–1832)
German writer and polymath

PURPOSE

» **Don't allow indecision to be your fate.**

» **Set the course.**

» **Release the handbrake.**

» **Be BOLD!**

This is where the proverbial rubber hits the road. You can choose to stay on your current path or you can choose to become an entrepreneur. You can choose to pursue your dreams or you can choose to work for someone who has followed their dreams.

Right now, your mind is racing with possibilities. Your wheels are spinning and you are creating a ton of noise and a ton of smoke, but you are not going anywhere. You are just wearing down your treads. Nothing happens until you release the handbrake.

No one feels 100% confident in releasing the handbrake. Many questions remain, such as: how fast will I take off, how hard will it be to steer, and can I handle the Gs? But unless you release the handbrake, nothing will happen. You are destined for more of the same. As author and speaker Tom Peters said, "Ready, Fire, Aim!" Don't wait to get it perfect before acting. Perfect never comes. If you pray for God to give you courage, he gives you the opportunity to be courageous. Action comes first, then growth. Entrepreneurs are not born, they are self-made.

Entrepreneurs know how to let go of the handbrake, even though questions remain. They make the best decision possible, knowing they will make corrections along the way.

What about you? What should you do? Should you hold tight or release the handbrake?

CALL UPON COURAGE

Through the exercises in this book, you have spent many hours collecting facts and examining details. Now you need to tuck away your notes and once again call upon your intuition. The facts you have gathered are your foundation. With your foundation in place, trust your intuition to send you in the right direction.

> "There is no scarcity of opportunity to make a living at what you want to do, there is only scarcity of resolve to make it happen."
>
> —Wayne Dyer (Born May 10, 1940), American self-help advocate, author, and lecturer

In order to make the right decision you need to courageously ask yourself one simple question: Which path gives me the best chance to achieve my vision? Answer this question and you will know what to do. Is it your current path or is it your target franchise? This is a rather simple question with profound consequences. Successful people have a determined focus. There will be challenges and setbacks along the way, but successful people know where they are going and are resolute in getting there. At this point, it can be assumed a certain amount of excitement, exhilaration, fear, and anxiety abounds. If fear and anxiety still cloud your thoughts, go back to the exercises in step 2. You have overcome fears in the past and you can do it again!

DEFINE YOUR FUTURE

Take some quiet time. Think about your future on each path. Use your intuition to direct your decision. Whatever your decision, it is time to **BE BOLD!** As your final exercise, rewrite your vision, this time adding your chosen path. Post it where it can serve as a continual reminder of your courage and drive. Then release the handbrake.

✏️ EXERCISE 15.1: FINAL VISION AND CHOSEN PATH

My future . . . _____

_____

_____

_____

_____

_____

_____

_____

_____

_____

_____

_____

_____

_____

_____

_____

_____

_____

_____

_____

_____

_____

_____

_____

_____

_____

_____

_____

_____

_____

_____

_____

_____

_____

_____

_____

_____

Throughout this workbook we have shared many wise words from the famous, the not-so-famous and even the unknown. Everyone needs a motto to live by. Capture how you feel right now and write your own life motto here:

> **"I promise . . .** to control my decision. I promise to be BOLD! I will not look back in twenty years and say, 'I wish I would have.' I promise to live a life reflective of my vision and a life by my design."
>
> X _____ X _____
>
> **Signature**   **Date**

Glossary of Franchise Terms

The following glossary of franchise terms has been meticulously constructed to be as accurate as possible. While some terms are based on generally accepted definitions, other terms may be subject to differing interpretations and uses. Franchising is an evolving and changing business format and, as such, the terminology used by its practitioners is similarly fluid. The intent of this glossary is to give the reader an introduction to some of the language used in franchising. It is not intended to be all inclusive but merely one tool to understanding this unique business format. We hope you find it useful.

A

Acknowledgement of Receipt
The final page of a **Franchise Disclosure Document (FDD)**, which, once signed and returned, confirms to the franchisor the date you received the document.

Advertising Co-op
A participatory body of **franchisees**—occasionally including the **franchisor**—that contributes money to a common fund to pay for regional or national advertising programs. Administration of advertising co-op funds varies from company to company. In most cases a committee of **franchisees** administer the fund. Alternatively, a special advertising committee made up of both **franchisees** and the **franchisor** may oversee use of the funds.

Advertising Commitment
This is an amount that a **franchisee** commits to spend on advertising and promotion in the local market. These monies are controlled by the individual **franchisee** and used to promote the **franchisee's** individual business.

Advertising Contribution
The monies that a **franchisee** is required to contribute to the **advertising fund** or the **advertising co-op**. These funds are used to pay for system-wide advertising and promotional expenses. The manner in which **advertising contributions** are made varies from company to company. Many **franchise agreements** specify a percentage of gross sales to be spent on advertising; the breakdown of expenditures for local, regional, and/or national advertising may also be specified.

Advertising Fee
Please see "**Advertising Contribution**."

Advertising Fund
Similar to an **advertising co-op**, this fund is administered and controlled by the **franchisor**.

Agent
A person authorized by another (often called a "principal") to act on his behalf.

Angel Investor
An individual or group of individuals who provide capital for a business start-up, usually in exchange for convertible debt or ownership equity. **Angel investors** invest their own personal funds, unlike **venture capital** firms that manage the pooled money of others in a managed fund. In some cases, if a family member or a friend were to lend you money to start a business, they also would be referred to as an **angel investor**.

Antitrust Law
Laws adopted to outlaw or restrict business practices considered monopolistic or that restrain trade. In the U.S., the principal **antitrust laws** are the Sherman Antitrust Act (enacted in 1890 and frequently amended), the Clayton Act (originally adopted in 1914), the Robinson-Patman Act (passed in 1936 to add price-discrimination prohibitions to the Clayton Act), and the Federal Trade Commission Act (also adopted in 1914). Some states have also adopted **antitrust laws**, such as the Donnelly Act in New York. Outside the U.S., antitrust laws are often referred to as "competition" laws.

Approval/Consent
In **franchising** this is a provision within the **franchise agreement** requiring that a party who wishes to act must obtain the consent or approval of the other party. For example, the **franchise agreement** may require that before the **franchisee** can transfer interest in the **franchise**, he/she must obtain "**approval/ consent**" of the **franchisor**.

Approved Supplier/Vendor
An **approved supplier/vendor** is an entity that has been approved by the **franchisor** to sell products and/or services to **franchisees** of its system. Items sold by **approved suppliers** may include equipment, ingredients, and other materials or items for use in operating the franchise business. The **franchisor** will generally approve several suppliers for each item and the **franchisee** may purchase the items from any of the **approved suppliers**. In some instances, a **franchisor** approves only one **approved supplier** of a specific product (i.e., a soft drink supplier) for purposes of system-wide uniformity. Also see "**Designated Supplier/ Vendor**."

Arbitration
In disputes between a **franchisee** and a **franchisor**, submitting the dispute for determination to private, unofficial persons or "arbitrators." Agreement to arbitrate must be stated, for example, in the **franchise agreement**, and **arbitration** findings are binding on both parties. A court's only basis for review of an arbitrator's decision is whether it was arbitrary, capricious, and an abuse of the arbitrator's discretion or beyond the arbitrator's authority.

GLOSSARY OF FRANCHISE TERMS

Area Developer

The **franchiso**r awards a single **franchisee** the right to operate more than one unit within a defined area, under a **development agreement** and based on an agreed-upon **development schedule**.

Area Representative

A type of **franchisee** that can own and operate **franchise outlets,** represent the **franchisor** in selling new **franchises**, and provide on-going local support to existing **franchisees** in a designated market. The **area representative** normally receives a portion of the **royalty fees** (and possibly the up-front **franchise fee**) payable by the **franchisees** to the **franchisor. Area representatives** may operate in a variety of geographical configurations, including metropolitan areas, a single state, or a combination of states. The **area representative** is not a party to the **franchise agreement**, which is between the **franchisor** and the **franchisee**. See, for comparison, "**Master Franchisee.**"

Assignment

Contractual authority of a **franchisee** to give away, sell, or otherwise transfer or dispose of all or certain ownership rights in the **franchise agreement**, the **franchised outlet,** and/or interest in the legal entity that owns the **franchise. Assignment** rights vary from **franchisor** to **franchisor** and may include the right to sell the business and transfer the **franchise agreement** to the buyer; or to transfer ownership and rights to the family; and/or for the estate to sell the **franchise** upon the owner's death or disability. Virtually all **franchise agreements** limit **assignment** in one way or another.

B

Bona Fide Wholesale Price

Defined in the **Federal Trade Commission's Franchise Rule** and one of three terms employed in defining a "**business format franchise.**" Refers to the price of goods or services for use by or to be made available for resale by the **franchisee**, the price of which is established in good faith without fraud or deceit. The **FTC Rule** provides that payments for the purchase of reasonable amounts of inventory at **bona fide wholesale prices** for resale or lease are not "required payments" and therefore are not considered the payment of a "**franchise fee.**" Also see "**Franchise.**"

Breakaway Franchisee

A **franchisee** who has unilaterally terminated their **franchise agreement**. Obligations of a **breakaway franchisee** may include some or all of the following: payment of substantial damages to the **franchisor**, resale of the business to the **franchisor**, or an obligation to abide by a post-term, non-compete covenant.

Bundle of Rights

All those rights and obligations that pass to the **franchisee** under the terms of a **franchise agreement**. These may include such items as right to use the **trade name**, right to knowledge of **trade secrets**, right to use the format of the business, right to build equity, and right to manage day-to-day operations in the prescribed manner.

Business Broker

An intermediary who manages the sale and/or purchase of an existing **franchised** business. Brokers can represent either sellers, buyers, or both. A **business broker** commonly, but not always, has a "**Fiduciary Duty**" within the relationship.

Business Format Franchising

The **franchising** system wherein the **franchisee** buys from the **franchisor** a total blueprint for doing business. Usually included is the license of a **trade name**, the **trademark**, access to **trade secrets**, and a clearly defined method and set of guidelines for conducting the business. Occasionally referred to as "**pure**" or "**comprehensive**" **franchising**.

Business Opportunity Laws

Laws regulating the sale of non-franchised "business opportunities." States that have such **business opportunity laws** typically exempt **franchise** programs that have federally registered **trade** or **service marks**, but some nonetheless require **franchisors** to file some form of application to claim that exemption. Some common business opportunities include vending machines, worm farming, envelope stuffing, and in-home mail order enterprises. In 2007, when it issued amendments to **the Franchise Rule**, the **FTC** also proposed a separate Business Opportunity Sales Regulation.

Business Plan

A **business plan** is a formal statement of a set of business goals, the reasons why they are believed attainable, and the plan for reaching those goals. It may also contain background information about the organization or team attempting to reach those goals.

Business Valuation

The practice of valuing an existing business. There are a large number of approaches to **Business Valuation**, including but not limited to Multiple of Earnings, Fair Market Value, Book Value, Replacement Value, Present Value, Future Value, Going Concern Value, Asset Value, Liquidation Value, etc.

Buy-back Option

A term of the **franchise agreement** wherein if the **franchisee** goes out of business the **franchisor** retains the right to buy back all assets at a pre-agreed price. The **buy-back** is an option that the **franchisor** retains and it is not a promise.

C

Camera-ready Advertising

Artwork and typeset materials that are ready for printing. **Camera-ready advertising** is for use in print media (newspapers, magazines, store signs, handbills, flyers, brochures, etc.). Since the cost of producing professional, **camera-ready advertising** is generally shared by all **franchisees**, the cost per **franchisee** is usually quite reasonable.

Cash/Initial Cash Required

One of a number of terms—the meanings of which vary from **franchisor** to **franchisor**—that are used to describe cash monies that the **franchisee** must spend prior to opening for business. Any of the following terms may be used in this context: cash required, initial cash required, **investment**, down payment, **equity investment**. Information concerning the **initial investment** that a prospective franchisee can expect to incur can be found in Item 7 of the **FDD**.

Cash-flow Projections

A spreadsheet that shows a month-by-month forecast of cash flow coming into the business and expected disbursements, including payroll, rent, insurance, debt, etc. A person considering entering into a business, including a franchise, should carefully examine their **cash-flow projections** to determine whether there will be adequate **working capital** for the new business.

Commitment Agreement

Please see "**Letter of Intent**."

Company-owned Outlet

In a **franchised** system, the outlets that are owned by the **franchisor** (or, sometimes, its affiliates).

Competing Operation

When a **franchisee** establishes, operates, owns, or has financial interest in any business that offers products or services the same or similar to those of the **franchise**, the **franchisee** may be said to have a "**competing operation**." Many **franchise agreements** restrict all **competing operations** during the term of the **franchise**; they may also restrict any competing activity or business after the term within a specific area and for a limited period (those parts of the **franchise agreement** are referred to as the "**non-compete clauses**").

Comprehensive Franchising

Please see "**Business Format Franchising**."

Conversion Franchising

The process by which existing independent businesses or dealers within an industry become **franchisees** when they assume the **trade name** and **trade dress** of the **franchisor**. **Conversion franchising** has been particularly widespread in the real estate industry.

Copyright

Generally, the exclusive right of the author or creator to protect his or her creation, such as a movie, book, music, or other expression. As it relates to **franchising**, **copyrights** most often apply to confidential written material (such as the **operating manual**, proprietary recipes, and the like). Under a **franchise agreement**, the **franchisor** usually licenses the **franchisee** to use those **copyrighted** materials in the operation of the **franchised** business for the term of the agreement.

Covenant of Good Faith / Fair Dealing

At the heart of a **franchise** is an agreement that sets out the essential contractual obligations governing the relationship between **franchisor** and the **franchisee**. The **franchise agreement**, however, cannot spell out all the obligations that a **franchisor** may owe the **franchisee**, and it has been argued that the **franchisor** also has an implied duty of "fair dealing" not contained explicitly in the **franchise agreement**. Courts usually find that the implied **covenant of good faith and fair dealing** cannot be used to contradict clear provisions in an agreement.

Covenants Against Competition

The clause or term of a **franchise agreement** in which the **franchisee** agrees not to engage in or maintain any interest in a business activity that competes with the **franchise** business. Also see "**Competing Operation**."

D

Decision-making Matrix

A knowledge-based tool found in *The Educated Franchisee* and this workbook to help support decision-making. This tool is focused on primary criteria and collected data and is central to a logic-based, decision-making approach.

Default

The neglect or failure of either party—**franchisee** or **franchisor**—to fulfill obligations and/or take the steps required under the **franchise agreement**.

Deferred Balance

A sum of money that the **franchisee** owes to the **franchisor**. A **deferred balance** is generally some remainder of the total amount initially paid for items such as equipment, fixtures, inventory, or construction/rent.

Demographics

A range of factors that may influence consumer behavior in a specific trade territory such as age, income, home prices, and socio-economic conditions.

Designated Supplier/Vendor

A designated entity from which **franchisees** are required to purchase certain products and/or services necessary to operate a **franchise** business. This usually applies to proprietary products and/or private label products manufactured to the **franchisor's** standards and specifications, but might also apply to other products that the **franchisor** believes are critical to the success of the **franchise** system. Also see "**Approved Supplier/Vendor**."

Development Agent

Please see "**Area Representative**."

Development Agreement

A term used to describe the agreement traditionally used to grant multi-unit **development rights** to **franchise developers** or **multi unit franchisees**. In the **development agreement**, the **franchisor** grants semi-exclusive "**development rights**" to a developer, which in turn agrees to establish a specific number of **franchised** units within a certain geographic area (called a "development area") in accordance with a predetermined "**development schedule**." Before the developer opens each **franchised** business, it typically is required to sign a **franchise agreement** for that **franchise**. The developer typically pays a "**development fee**" to the **franchisor**, a portion of which may be credited toward the **initial franchise fee** due under the unit **franchise agreements**.

Development Fee

Please see "**Development Agreement**."

Development Rights

Please see "**Development Agreement**."

Development Schedule

Please see "**Development Agreement**."

Disclosure Document
Currently required under the laws of fifteen states, a **disclosure document** is provided by the **franchisor** to a prospective **franchisee**. The document contains information about the **franchisor**, the **franchise** being offered, and the terms and conditions of the legal relationship into which the **franchisee** will enter. The state agency that administers the **franchise** laws typically reviews the document and other pertinent materials the **franchisor** will use in promoting the sale of the **franchise**. Also see "**Franchise Disclosure Document** ."

Discovery Day
An event set up by the **franchisor** so that potential franchisees may learn more about becoming a **franchisee**. A **discovery day** typically takes place at the **franchisors** headquarters and is often the final step in the **due diligence** process. It provides the opportunity to meet the management team, support team, and trainers face-to-face. Occasionally called "Meet The Team Day" or "Open House."

Discrimination
Treating one **franchisee** differently from another. A number of statutes and legal cases restrict a **franchisor's** ability to discriminate among businesses that are similarly situated.

Distributor
An individual or company through whom a manufacturer sells his products to retailers and/or consumers. Conventional **distributors** may handle several lines of competing products, whereas franchised distributors typically only handle the products of one **franchisor**. Franchised distributors operate exactly as other independently-owned, franchised businesses, receiving training, management, and advertising support from the **franchisor**.

Downpayment
Please see "**Cash/Initial Cash Required**."

Dual Distribution
When a **franchisor** operates **company-owned outlet** on the same marketing level as its **franchisees**.

Due Diligence
Usually undertaken by investors, but also customers, **due diligence** refers to the process of making sure that someone is what they say they are and can do what they claim; i.e., investigation of a business (e.g., Does the product or system really work? Does the franchise really have customers?).

E

Earnings Claim
Please see "**Financial Performance Representation**."

Encroachment
Any **franchisee**—or the **franchisor**—attempting to sell products or services within an area of territory that has been assigned to or designated exclusively for another owner.

Entrepreneur
A person who is willing to assume the responsibility, risk, and rewards of starting and operating a business.

Equity Interest

Any legal ownership of the **franchise** business or the corporation that owns the **franchise** business.

Estimated Initial Investment
A detailed listing of all fees and expenses you should expect to incur in starting a **franchised** business. This listing represents the total amount that a **franchisee** would need to pay or get financed, including fees paid to the **franchisor** and goods/services purchased from third parties. This estimate can be found in Item 7 of the **Franchise Disclosure Document**.

Exclusive Territory
A territory assigned to a **franchisee** within which a **franchisor** agrees not to operate a **facility** (or grant a license to another party to operate a **facility**) that is the same as the franchised business, under the same marks, and under the same system. Most **franchisors** reserve rights with respect to other methods of distributing products or services (such as internet sales). Not all **franchisors** offer **exclusive territories**.

Expiration of Term
In a **franchise agreement**, the date upon which the contract expires if it is not renewed.

F

Facility
Please see "**Site**."

FDD
Please See "**Franchise Disclosure Document**"

Federal Trade Commission (FTC)
An independent agency of the United States government headed by five commissioners, each of whom is appointed to office by the president and confirmed by the U.S. Senate. The president has the authority to designate one of the commissioners as chairman of the agency. The **FTC** has an extensive staff and is charged with administering and enforcing the **Franchise Rule** as well as general prohibitions against unfair and deceptive practices; for example, involving advertising.

Fiduciary Duty
A requirement that a person act toward others and the public with the watchfulness, attention, caution, and prudence that a reasonable person in the circumstances would use.

Field Representative
Please see "**Franchise Representative**."

Financial Forecast
Please see "**Financial Performance Representation**."

Financial Performance Representation
Any oral, visual, or written representation to a prospective **franchisee** or for general dissemination in the media which states or suggests a specific level or range of potential or actual sales, income, gross, or net profit. This information must be provided in Item 19 of the **Franchise Disclosure Document**. Previously called "**Earnings Claim.**"

First Personal Meeting
Historically the **Federal Trade Commission** required **franchisors** and their sales representatives to provide the **Federal Trade Commission Disclosure Document** to the prospective **franchisees** during the **first personal meeting**. This requirement was eliminated in the 2007 amendments to **the FTC Rule**. Two states have retained this requirement. Please see "**Reasonable Request.**"

Forum Selection
A term in the **franchise agreement** that designates the state and court in which disputes are to be litigated.

Fractional Franchise
A relationship that is exempted from the **FTC Rule** because the **franchisee** or its principals have had more than two years of prior experience in the **franchised** or similar business; and wherein the **franchisor** or the **franchisee** anticipates that the **franchisee's** sales arising from the **franchise** would represent no more than 20% of projected volume in the first year of the relationship. Some **state franchise laws** also have a **fractional franchise** exemption.

Franchise
The **FTC Franchise Rule** defines a "franchise" as an arrangement whereby a **franchisor** grants **franchisees** the right to operate a business that: 1) is identified with the **franchisor's trademark**; 2) is subject to the **franchisor's** significant control and/or assistance; and 3) in exchange for which, the **franchisee** pays a "**franchise fee**" to the **franchisor** or its affiliate. Most **state franchise laws** adopt a similar definition (except in New York, where any combination of elements 1 and 3, or elements 2 and 3, are enough to satisfy the state law definition of "franchise").

Franchise Agreement/Contract
The legal document that sets forth the rights and obligations of the **franchisee** and the **franchisor**. Commonly included is information about territory, location, training, management, **renewal**, **termination**, dispute resolution, suppliers, **quality control**, product standards, advertising, etc.

Franchise Broker
Please see "**Franchise Consultant.**"

Franchise Company
Please see "**Franchisor.**"

Franchise Consultant
An independent **agent** or middleman who acts as an intermediary between the **franchisor** and a prospective **franchisee**. **Franchise consultants** are commonly paid on a success basis by the **franchisor**. As **agents** of the **franchisor**, **franchise consultants** are required to act in accordance with all laws and regulations governing the sale of **franchises**.

Franchise Disclosure Document
The **Franchise Disclosure Document (FDD)** is the form for providing disclosure in the U.S. under the **FTC Franchise Rule**. Before the 2007 amendments to the **FTC Franchise Rule**, the principal format for providing disclosure in the U.S. was a document prepared under the "**Uniform Franchise Offering Circular**" (**UFOC**) format. The **FDD** provides extensive information about the **franchisor** and the franchise organization in a uniform format, which a prospective **franchisee** can use to compare different franchise offerings. The FDD is meant to give a potential **franchisee** certain specified information to help make educated decisions about their potential investments. Also see "**Disclosure Document**" and "**FTC Franchise Rule.**"

Franchise Disclosure Laws
Federal and State laws that require a **franchisor** to deliver a **franchise disclosure document** ("**FDD**") to a prospective **franchisee** prior to selling a **franchise** to the prospect. See "**FTC Franchise Rule**" and "**State Franchise Disclosure Laws.**"

Franchise Fee
A sum of money the **franchisee** pays to the **franchisor** when the **franchise agreement** is signed. The fee may cover a variety of expenses, including but not limited to training costs, on-site startup costs, and promotional charges. Also called a "**License Fee**" or "**Initial Fee.**"

Franchise Owner
Please see "**Franchisee.**"

Franchise Relationship Laws
State laws regulating certain aspects of the **franchise** relationship, such as how and when a **franchisor** can terminate the **franchise agreement**, where lawsuits concerning the **franchise** relationship must be brought, and the circumstances under which a **franchisor** can refuse to permit the **franchisee** to renew the **franchise agreement**.

Franchise Representative
An employee of the **franchisor** whose responsibility it is to regularly visit with and assist **franchisees** within an assigned geographic area. **Franchise representatives**, also called **field representatives**, may inspect locations for quality and cleanliness; help **franchisees** solve management or technical problems; troubleshoot; give moral support; act as liaison between **franchise** owner and **franchise** company; and offer advertising and marketing advice.

Franchise Rule
Please see "**FTC Franchise Rule.**"

Franchise Sales Material

Promotional and/or instructional materials made available to individuals who inquire about purchasing a **franchise**. Such "kits" commonly contain **disclosure documents**, a description of the business and history of the company, financial information, testimonials from current **franchise owners**, preliminary information about fees and costs, etc.

Franchise Salesperson

An **agent** of the **franchisor** whose business it is to market and sell **franchises**. The franchise salesperson's role is to meet with prospective **franchisees,** present disclosure materials, gather the prospect's financial information, answer questions, assist with obtaining financing, and facilitate the signing of a **franchise agreement**.

Franchise Term

The length of time for which a **franchisee** is granted licensing and other rights under the **franchise agreement**.

Franchised Outlet/Unit

Within a **franchise** system, a business location or **site** that is independently owned by an individual(s) to whom the **franchisor** has granted certain rights. For comparison see "**company-owned outlet**."

Franchisee

The individual or individuals who own and operate a business under a licensing agreement granted by a parent company known as the **franchisor**. **Franchisees** are commonly are entitled to: use the **franchisor's trademark** and/or **trade name**; sell and/or market the **franchisor's** products and/or services; have access to the **franchisor's** pertinent **trade secrets**; receive management and other training; enjoy marketing and advertising support; build **equity interest** in the business; and benefit from the **goodwill** of the **franchisor**. **Franchisees** can also be called "**Franchise Owners**."

Franchisee Advisory Board

A **franchisor**-sponsored organization of **franchisees**, either appointed by the **franchisor** and/or elected from among the **franchisees** at large, who represent or speak for the **franchisees** in discussions with the **franchisor**. Practices vary but **franchise advisory boards** may, with the approval of all **franchisees**, levy assessments; run marketing, advertising, and training programs; and represent grievances to the **franchisor**. Also called "Franchisee Advisory Council."

Franchisee Association

An independent association of **franchisees** who work together to address the issues that affect all **franchisees** within a given **franchise** system. **Franchisee Associations** generally speak for all **franchisees** who have chosen to join the association and are independent of, and not directed by, the **franchisor**. Also see "**Franchisee Advisory Board**."

Franchisee/Franchisor Relations

Refers to the manner in which **franchisee** and **franchisor** representatives interact. Such relations may be generally positive and cooperative or they may encounter periods of stress and distrust. To ensure smooth **franchisee/franchisor relations**, many **franchisors** have established **franchise advisory boards** comprised of **franchisees** who meet regularly with company representatives. Also see "**Franchisee Advisory Board**."

Franchisee Training

Education and instruction on how to properly run the business, which the **franchisor** provides to the **franchisee** after the **franchise agreement** is signed. The training may be provided as part of the **initial fee** or may be an added expense for the **franchisee**. The training may take place at the **franchisor's** training facility, at the **franchisee's** actual business location, or both.

Franchisee Validation

During the process of investigating a **franchise** opportunity a prospective **franchisee** will interview current and past **franchisees**, obtaining unfiltered opinions about the quality of the **franchise** system.

Franchising

A method of marketing products and/or services under which a **franchisor** licenses its **trademark** and operating system and/or know-how to a **franchisee** in exchange for both on-going fees paid by the **franchisee** to the **franchisor** during the term of the **franchise** and the **franchisee's** agreement to follow the **franchisor's** standards and specifications for the **franchise** system. **Franchise** arrangements have been subdivided into two broad classes: 1) Product distribution arrangements in which the dealer is to some degree, but not entirely, identified with the manufacturer/ supplier; and 2) entire **business format franchising**, in which there is complete identification of the dealer with the buyer.

Franchisor

The **franchisor** owns the business system and associated **trademarks** or **trade names**. **Franchisor**s allow **franchisees** to use these under license in a designated area and for a fee. They then support their **franchisees** both in starting their business and in continued support. Also called "**Franchise Company**."

FTC Advisory Opinion

A finding of the **Federal Trade Commission** that addresses the propriety of certain **franchise** business practices and delivers an opinion on whether or not the practices conform with the **FTC's** "**Franchise Trade Rule**." The **FTC's** staff also issues informal staff advisory opinions that are not binding, but that give guidance about how the **FTC's** enforcement staff thinks about a particular fact pattern.

FTC Disclosure Document

Please see "**Franchise Disclosure Document**."

FTC Franchise Rule

A nationwide regulation issued by the **Federal Trade Commission** that principally requires **franchisors** to provide disclosure to prospective **franchisees**. The **FTC Franchise Rule** requires disclosure in the form of a "**Franchise Disclosure Document**" (or "**FDD**"). The **FTC Franchise Rule** was issued in 1978 and took effect in 1979; the regulation was extensively amended in 2007. There is no requirement to file the **FDD** with the **FTC**.

Full-Time Work Requirement

This is a **franchise** system with a **franchise agreement** that requires the **franchisee** to be involved in the daily operations of the business on a full-time basis.

G

Good Cause
In **franchising**, "**good cause**" is commonly invoked as legally sufficient grounds or reason to support the actions of one or the other party, particularly in the case of nonrenewal or **termination** of the **franchise agreement**.

Goodwill
The positive reputation or image that a **franchisor** has earned from the public. Although **goodwill** cannot be measured in precise monetary terms, image, reputation, public awareness, and acceptance all contribute to a company's value or worth. Typically, the **goodwill** associated with a **trademark** does not legally transfer to the **franchisee**.

Gross Sales
Total value of all sales prior to adjusting for costs or discounting.

Group Purchasing Power
In **franchising**, the ability of a group of store operators, including **franchisees** and company-owned units, to obtain a lower price for goods and materials when such goods and materials are purchased in large quantity. Also implied is the groups' greater influence with the supplier in terms of timely delivery, service, and so on.

Guarantee
A promise or assurance, especially one in writing, that something is of specified quality, content, or benefit; or that it will perform satisfactorily for a given length of time.

H

Household Cash Flow
Total household income minus total household expenses over a predetermined period of time.

I

Independent Contractor
For tax and legal purposes, an individual who is not classified as an employee but who is deemed to be in business for him- or herself.

Infringement
A trespass or **encroachment** upon one's rights; used especially in relation to invasions of the rights secured by patents, **copyrights**, and **trademarks**.

Initial Fee
Please see "**Franchise Fee**."

Initial Investment
The required amount of money required for a new **franchisee** to open and operate a location for at least three months. This must include all "start-up" expenses, but may not be reflective of total investment. Information about a prospective **franchisee's initial Investment** can be found in Item 7 of the **Franchise Disclosure Document**.

Injunction
A judicial process or order requiring the person(s) to whom it is directed to do a particular act or to refrain from doing a particular act.

International Franchise Association (IFA)
The **International Franchise Association** is the world's oldest and largest organization representing **franchising** worldwide. In 2010, the **IFA** celebrated 50 years of excellence, education, and advocacy. The **IFA** protects, enhances, and promotes **franchising** through government relations, public relations, and educational programs. **IFA** members include **franchise** companies in over 90 different business format categories, individual **franchisees**, and companies that support the industry in marketing, law, and business development.

International Franchising
Refers to the expansion of **franchising** beyond national borders. A growing number of **franchisors** are currently operating **franchised** and/or **company-owned outlets** outside their home country.

Investment/Equity Investment
Please see "**Cash/Initial Cash Required**."

J

Joint and Several Liability
Where multiple parties, such as shareholders or parties owning a **franchised** unit, share equal financial and legal responsibilities and therefore are together subject to any and all lawsuits or legal actions filed by creditors or other plaintiffs.

K

L

Lanham Act
A shortened name for the United States Trademark Act of 1946.

Lease Security Payment
A payment made to the individual(s) who grants a lease on the property where a **franchise** is located. The **lease security payment** is most often paid by the **franchisee** to protect the leaseholder against losses in case of business failure or **default**.

Letter of Intent
A written statement of intention to perform an act. In **franchising**, the **franchisor** sometimes provides to the prospective **franchisee** a **letter of intent** stating the company's intention to offer a **franchise agreement**. In commercial banking practices, a **letter of intent**, or **commitment agreement**, may state the bank's intention to make a loan to the prospective **franchisee**. **Letters of intent** are usually not binding legal commitments.

License Fee
Please see "**Franchise Fee**."

Licensee
Please see "**Licensor**."

Licensor
In **franchising**, another term for "**franchisor**." The term is also used to describe the party who grants another the right to use its **trademark** in connection with the sale of the **licensor's** products without the use of the **licensor's** operating system.

Liquid Assets
Please see "**Liquid Capital**."

Liquid Capital
Assets held in cash or in something that can be readily turned into cash. Also known as "**Liquid Assets**."

Location
Please see "**Site**."

Logotype
A **franchisor's trademark** or name, as it is distinctively designed or written.

M

Management Fee
A sum of money the **franchisee** pays for continuing management aid and assistance. Such fees may be included in the royalty or service fee or may be an additional charge.

Manager Operated/Run
A **franchise** system that does not require the **franchisee** to be personally involved in the daily operations of the **franchised unit** on a full-time basis. An operation that is well suited for investors and part-time involvement.

Marketing Plan
Generally, a **marketing plan** is a written document that details the necessary actions to achieve one or more marketing objectives. In regard to franchising, the marketing plan is a term that is often used as a short-hand way of describing the second element of the term "**franchise**" under the **FTC's Franchise Rule.** Please also see "**Franchise**."

Master Franchisee
A system whereby a **franchisor** grants to a party (usually referred to as the **Master Franchisee**) the right to operate **franchised** businesses and to grant **sub-franchises** to third parties, within an agreed-upon geographic area. The **Master Franchisee** serves as if it were the "**franchisor**" within the **sub-franchise** territory, providing localized support services within the territory. The **Master Franchisee** typically retains a portion of the royalty as compensation for its services.

Maximum Investment Level
Maximum dollar amount an investor is both comfortable and qualified investing (cash and borrowed) into a business. This amount generally includes both cash and debt.

Minority Business Enterprise (MBE)
An **MBE** is a business that is typically majority-owned and controlled by U.S. citizens who are members of certain defined minority groups. Some **MBEs** may be granted preferences in terms of obtaining **contracts**, for example, when municipalities control a venue, such as an airport concession authority on toll roads, etc.

Multiunit Franchisee

A **franchisee** that owns and operates more than one **franchised** location.

Mutual Evaluation Process

The understanding that both the **franchisor** and the prospective **franchisee** are evaluating each other during the due-diligence process to determine if it would be mutually beneficial to move forward into a **franchise** relationship.

N

Net Worth

An individual's total assets minus their total liabilities.

Non-compete Clause

The provision in a **franchise agreement** which prohibits a **franchisee** from owning, operating, or having an interest in any competing business offering the same or similar products or services as those provided by the **franchise**. A **non-competition clause** may also prohibit the **franchisee** from involvement in any such competing business for a specified length of time following nonrenewal or **termination** of the **franchise agreement**. Also called "**Non-Competition Clause**".

O

Offering Circular

Please see "**Franchise Disclosure Document**."

Offering Prospectus

Please see "**Franchise Disclosure Document**."

Opening Costs

Total **franchisee** cost to start the business and remain operating for a reasonable period (typically defined as three months). **Opening costs** may include **franchise fees**, costs of real estate and or rent, zoning and business licenses, financing expenses, inventory expense, equipment, training fees, **working capital**, payroll, insurance, and salaries for employees. Please see "**Cash/Initial Cash Required**."

Operating Controls

Please see "**Quality Control**."

Operations Manual

The document detailing the operation of a particular **franchised** business. **Operations manuals**—also called **franchise** manuals—describe such items as: **quality control** requirements; recommended hours of operation and financial and management practices; the correct use of any **trademarks** or **trade names**; forms and written materials for use in business operations; payment of fees and **royalties**; approved suppliers; and so on. Increasingly, **operations manuals** also address other matters, such as systemwide policies concerning data, environmental and energy standards, health and safety matters, etc.

Owner Benefit

This is a descriptive term that describes business income minus all "true" business expenses. Any benefit a **franchisee** receives from the business—either through pass-through expenses, retirement contributions, dividends, distributions, or salary—is considered part of **Owner Benefit**. Other terms include "Owners Discretionary Profit" or "Earnings Before Interest Taxes Depreciation and Amortization (EBITDA) Plus Add-Backs."

P

Per Se
When used in **antitrust law**, a **"per se"** violation is one that is inherently illegal once proven.

Personal Living Expenses
The amount of money required for you and your family to live. Also called "Family Expenses."

Pre-opening Promotion
Special marketing, promotion, or advertising that precedes by some length of time the opening of a new **franchised** or **company-owned outlet**. **Pre-opening promotion** heightens consumer awareness and puts the new business on sound footing.

Preferred Lender
A lender that specializes in franchise financing and has a pre-existing relationship with a target **franchisor**.

Price Fixing
A criminal violation of federal antitrust statues in which several competing businesses reach a secret agreement (conspiracy) to set prices for their products or prevent real competition and keep the public from benefiting from the competition. "Horizontal **price fixing**" among competitors at the same level of commerce (for example, two or more **franchisees**) is typically "**per se**" illegal. Under a series of decisions reached by the U.S. Supreme Court, parties such as **franchisors** are permitted to specify a maximum and a minimum resale price, which may still be reviewed under federal **antitrust law** under the "**rule of reason**" standard.

Principal Register
The U.S. Patent and Trademark Office (USPTO) maintains a list of all **registered trademarks**. The USPTO list includes the "Principal Register." When a **trademark** is listed on the **Principal Register**, it puts all parties in the country on constructive notice of the **registration** as well as the registrant's use of the mark. When a mark has been included on the **Principal Register**, the owner of that mark is entitled to exercise all of the rights provided by the U.S. Trademark Act.

Product Liability
In **franchising**, the term implies the risk assumed by **franchisor** and **franchisee** in providing the **franchised** goods and/or services to the consuming public.

Product Specifications
Commonly spelled out in the **operations manual**, **product specifications** are precise and detailed descriptions and/or designations of ingredients, materials, goods, and other items used in the operation of the business.

Product Standardization

Related to **quality control**, **product standardization** is the **franchisor's** effort to provide in every **franchised** and **company-owned outlet**, goods and/or services which are uniform in quality, appearance, and character.

Profit Projections

Please see "**Financial Performance Representation**."

Prospectus

Please see "**Franchise Disclosure Document**."

Protected Area

Please see "**Exclusive Territory**."

Protected Territory

Please see "**Exclusive Territory**."

Public Offering Prospectus

Please see "**Franchise Disclosure Document**."

Purchasing Power

Please see "**Group Purchasing Power**."

Pure Franchising

Please see "**Business Format Franchising.**"

Q

Quality Control

The practices of a **franchisor** in supervising, regulating, and directing how business will be conducted in a **franchised** or **company-owned outlet**. Strict **quality control** is the **franchisor's** most important method of insuring a uniform high-quality of product and services in all outlets. **Trademark** owners are required, under the U.S. Trademark Act, to police their marks and the products and services sold under those marks.

R

Reasonable Request

Under the **Federal Trade Commission Rule**, **franchisors** and their sales representatives are required to provide the **Franchise Disclosure Document** to a prospective **franchisee** upon **reasonable request**. When the **FTC** issued the amended **FTC Rule** in 2007, the agency declined to provide a specific definition for the term "**reasonable request**," noting instead that "determinations about 'reasonableness' can be made only on a case-by-case basis."

Registration

In those states that have a state **franchise** law, **franchisors** must file an application to register before offering and selling **franchises** in that state. In some of these states, the application consists of filing a copy of the **franchisor's FDD** as well as certain additional forms. State **registration** applications typically are part of the public record.

Registration State

A state where there is a "**state franchise law**." Currently CA, HA, IL, IN, MD, MI, MN, NY, ND, OR, RI, SD, VA, WA, WI. See "**State Franchise Laws**."

Relevant Market

A way of identifying a market area according to its geography. In **franchising**, the term usually identifies the area in which a particular business entity has control.

Renewable Option

Please see "**Renewal**."

Renewal

Most **franchise agreements** are for a specified period of time; at the end of that period the **franchisee** generally has the option to **renew** at a specified fee and upon signing the then current **franchise agreement**. The **franchise agreement** presented at **renewal** time may be substantially different from the one originally signed; for example, the **royalties** and **advertising fees** may be higher.

Right of First Refusal

A **franchisee's** contractual right to purchase—if he so decides and if he can meet all conditions of sale established by the **franchisor**—any additional **franchised outlets** that may be for sale in the future within a pre-defined territory. This can also apply to a **franchisor's** right to repurchase a **franchised unit** at the same price as offered by a third party.

Royalty Fee

A regular and continuing payment made by the **franchisee** to the **franchisor**, often paid on a weekly or monthly basis. The **royalty** may be a percentage of sales, a fixed recurring fee, or a combination. **Royalties** commonly cover use of a **trademark** and **trade name** and also constitute a fee for services performed by the **franchisor** such as training and assistance, marketing, advertising, accounting, and so on. Also called "**service fees**" and/or "**license fees**."

Rule of Reason

Under federal **antitrust law**, a method for judging illegality. Under the laws, certain practices are presumed to be illegal "**per se**" without regard to the precise harm they have caused or the business justification for their use. Other practices are judged under the "**Rule of Reason**," under which the practices are generally deemed illegal only if, on balance, they harm competition. Also see "**Antitrust Law**."

S

SBA Certified Bank

Commercial banks which have applied for and been accepted to participate in the U.S. Small Business Administration's loan **guarantee** program. (Also see **SBA guaranteed loan**). While any commercial lending institution may utilize the **SBA guaranteed loan** program, such Certified Banks are more likely to be familiar with the program, thus facilitating approval of the application.

SBA Guaranteed Loan
A program of financial assistance available to small business owners from the U.S. Small Business Administration (SBA). While the SBA seldom loans money directly to **franchisees**, an **SBA guaranteed loan** makes it easier for a qualified individual to borrow money from a commercial lending institution, such as a bank. Under the program, the loan is made directly by the bank to the **franchisee**. The SBA protects the bank against financial loss in the event of business failure.

Service Fees
Please see "**Royalty Fee**."

Service Franchising
A type of **franchising** which primarily provides a service, assistance or advice to the consumer. Service **franchises** are typically **business format franchises** and include, but are not limited to, the following: tax preparation, accounting, haircutting, staffing, window-washing, business coaching, real estate, maid services, dry cleaning, painting, etc.

Service Mark
Marks used to identify services, rather than goods, and used in the same fashion as **trademarks**. Also see "**Trademarks**."

Site
The specific premises from which the **franchisee** is to conduct business. Also called "location" and "facility."

Site Selection
The process of choosing the location for a **franchised** business. Professional **site selection** involves knowledge of such considerations as **demographics**, traffic patterns, buying habits, market characteristics, wage and employment patterns, zoning and other land use regulations, building and health code ordinances, and real estate patterns.

Standardized Operating Procedures
Please see "**Operating Controls**."

Start-up Costs
Please see "Initial Investment."

State Addendum
Refers to an additional document that contains additional disclosures required by a **registration state**. State addenda are added into the **FDD** as exhibits.

State Franchise Laws
In some states, a law requires **franchisors** to comply with certain requirements in addition to the **FTC Franchise Rule**. Typically, **state franchise laws** require a **franchisor** to do two things: 1) register with the state each year before starting to offer **franchises**; and 2) give disclosure. While most of these states have agreed to allow **franchisors** to use the **FDD** for providing disclosure, some states require slight changes or modifications to the **FDD**, which are accomplished through the use of state addenda and state amendments.

Sub Franchisor
Please see "**Master Franchisee**."

Supplemental Register

This is the secondary **trademark** register for the United States Patent and Trademark Office (USPTO). It allows for **registration** of certain marks that are not eligible for **registration** on the **Principal Register**, but are capable of distinguishing an applicant's goods or services. Marks registered on the **Supplemental Register** receive protection from conflicting marks and other protections, but are excluded from receiving the advantages of certain sections of the Trademark Act of 1946.

T

Termination

A declaration by the **franchisor** that part or all of the rights and obligations—of both parties—under the **franchise contract** cease or have ceased as of a certain date. Certain responsibilities and/or claims and damages may survive this **termination**, however. The conditions under which a **franchise** may be terminated by the **franchisor** are commonly addressed to in the **franchise agreement.**

Termination Legislation

A number of states have passed **franchise** relationship laws which govern the reasons for and manner by which a **franchisor** may terminate or fail to renew a **franchise agreement**. Such so-called "**termination/ non-renewal legislation**" also has been proposed in Congress from time-to time but has never been passed into law. Regulations regarding **termination** and nonrenewal therefore differ from state-to-state.

Territorial Restrictions

Please see "**Exclusive Territory**."

Total Investment

Please see "**Initial Investment**."

Trade Dress

A term that refers to the visual appearance of an item, such as the interior or exterior of a building or a product's packaging. Typically, **trade dress** denotes some distinctive quality or look that is not functional, and that signals to consumers that the products, services, or the establishment is associated with a particular brand. The overall visual manner in which a **franchise** business presents itself to the public, including the interior and exterior design of buildings, its choice of color, use of dress of its employees, and so on.

Trademark

Any word, name, symbol, or device or any combination thereof adopted and used by a **franchisor** to identify its goods and/or services and distinguish them from those manufactured or sold by others. A careful **franchisor** grants only clearly defined or restricted use of its **trademark**. Such restrictions are spelled out in the **franchise agreement** and are therefore commonly referred to as "contractually limited use" of the **trademark**.

Trade name

Individual names and surnames, firm names, and **trade names** used by **franchise** companies to identify their business.

Trade Secret

A process, method, plan, formula, or other information unique to a **franchisor** that gives it an advantage over competitors. Appropriate legal provisions written into the **franchise agreement**, such as a **covenant not to compete**, are important in protecting **trade secrets**.

Training Cost/Expense

The money a **franchisee** pays for education and instruction. Training expenses may or may not include such items as: travel to and from the training location; room and board during training; the cost of tuition, books and supplies; and on-site startup aid. Practices vary, but training costs may be covered by the **franchise fee**.

Transfer Rights

Please see "**Assignment**."

Turn-key Operation

A term used to describe a **franchise** that is so thoroughly organized, fully equipped, and professionally set up that the new **franchisee** need only "turn the key" in order to commence business.

Tying

Under **antitrust law**, **tying** is a requirement imposed upon a buyer to purchase one product on the condition that the buyer also buy another product from the same seller. Whether alleged "**tying**" is illegal under **antitrust law** is often based on the facts of a particular case, and claims of **tying** are typically judged under the "**rule of reason**" standard.

U

Uniform Franchise Offering Circular (UFOC)

This term is no longer used. Please see "**Franchise Disclosure Document** "

Unilateral Termination

Wherein one of the parties to the **franchise agreement** decides, without the other's agreement, to put an end to the business relationship. **Unilateral termination** may be allowable with "**good cause**" and/or for pre-agreed reasons spelled out in the **franchise agreement**. Either the **franchisor** or the **franchisee** may seek to unilaterally terminate a **contract**; whether or not it is legal to do so will depend on circumstances and on the terms of the **contract**.

V

Variable Cost

Any costs that change significantly with the level of output, such as material costs.

Venture Capital

A person or group of individuals who invest in a business venture, providing capital for start-up or expansion. **Venture capitalists** are looking for a higher rate of return than would be given by more traditional **investments**.

Vertical Restraints

Restrictions imposed by a **franchisor** on its "downstream" customer or **franchisee**. An example of such restraint may be a limitation on where a **franchisee** may offer and sell products or services. Also see "**Price Fixing**."

Vicarious Liability

In **franchising**, "**vicarious liability**" typically refers to claims brought against a **franchisor** alleging that it is responsible for the action (or inaction) of a **franchisee** or one of its **franchisee's** employees or **agents**.

Vision Statement

A well-written **vision statement** will provide both direction and motivation to help you move toward a better future of your design. A well-developed **vision statement** includes measurement standards and target dates.

W

Waiver

In a typical **franchise agreement**, there is an "anti-waiver" clause, which states that one party's acceptance of late performance or non-performance of an obligation by the other party does not waive the requirement that the same obligation be met in the future.

Working Capital

A financial metric that represents liquidity available to a business or organization. A company can have both assets and profit but be short of liquidity if its assets cannot readily be converted into cash. Positive **working capital** is required to ensure that a firm is able to continue its operations and that it has sufficient funds to satisfy both maturing short-term debt and upcoming operational expenses.

GLOSSARY SOURCES

Thanks must be given for the substantial assistance received from:

- The International Franchise Association (www.Franchise.org)

- *The Educated Franchisee* (www.EducatedFranchisee.com)

- Kenneth S. Kaplan, General Counsel, Fantastic Sam's International

- Lee Plave, CFE, Partner, Plave Koch PLC

Additional sources include, but are not limited to, www.Webster.com and www.Wikipedia.com.

Resources

Consulting Organizations

http://www.educatedfranchisee.com/
franchise-consulting-organizations.aspx

Directory of Franchises

http://www.entrepreneur.com/franchises/
index.html

Entrepreneur Fear Box

http://www.educatedfranchisee.com/
download-center.aspx

Finance Option Summary

http://www.educatedfranchisee.com/
download-center.aspx

Franchise Finance Organizations

http://www.educatedfranchisee.com/
franchise-funding.aspx

Franchise Industry Research

http://www.educatedfranchisee.com/
download-center.aspx

Franchise Website List

http://www.educatedfranchisee.com/
franchise-opportunity.aspx

Free Credit Report Website

http://www.annualcreditreport.com

International Franchise Association

http://www.franchise.org

Retirement Planning Calculator

http://www.aarp.org/work/retirement-
planning/retirement_nest_egg_calculator/

Sample Questions for Franchisees

http://www.educatedfranchisee.com/
download-center.aspx

Bibliography

The Educated Franchisee: The How-To Book for Choosing a Winning Franchise. Rick Bisio (written with Mike Kohler. Bascom Hill Publishing Group, Minneapolis, MN (2008).

Blink: The Power of Thinking without Thinking. Malcolm Gladwell. Little Brown and Company, New York, NY (2005).

Feel the Fear and Do It Anyway. Susan Jeffers, PhD. Random House Publishing Group, New York (1987).

How We Decide. Jonah Lehrer. Houghton Mifflin Harcourt, New York, NY (2009).

Loopholes of the Rich: How the Rich Legally Make More Money & Pay Less Tax. Diane Kennedy, CPA. John Wiley & Sons, Inc., Hoboken, NJ (2005).

Rich Dad, Poor Dad: What the Rich Teach Their Kids About Money—That the Poor and Middle Class Do Not!. Robert T. Kiyosaki. Warner Books, New York, NY (1997).

The Millionaire Next Door: The Surprising Secrets of America's Wealthy. Thomas J. Stanley, Ph.D. and William D. Danko, Ph.D. Simon & Schuster, New York, NY (1996).

About the Authors

This time-proven workbook leverages forty years of franchise experience. The authors are widely respected as exceptional franchise consultants and spend thousands of hours every year directly helping individuals, partnerships and investor groups to identify the perfect franchise. Below, please find a brief summary of each of the authors. Should you have questions about franchising or if you wish to discuss your personal situation directly with either author, please find their contact information below. They look forward to hearing from you.

RICK BISIO

In today's world of "instant experts," Rick Bisio truly stands apart. Mr. Bisio has dedicated his life to business ownership and franchising.

As an author, Mr. Bisio has written the highly acclaimed *The Educated Franchisee*, now in its third edition. This book has been exceptionally helpful to the thousands of people who are currently exploring franchising. *The Educated Franchisee* is consistently ranked as one of the best-selling franchising books in the country.

As a franchise consultant, Mr. Bisio is widely recognized as one of the best, having successfully worked with thousands of individuals to help them identify the perfect franchise. Mr. Bisio guides his clients through an eye-opening process of self-discovery. Mr. Bisio's uncanny ability to identify each person's unique interests, skills, and abilities has resulted in thousands of great business decisions across a wide range of industries.

As an entrepreneur, Mr. Bisio has owned both franchised and non-franchised businesses. Having owned successful businesses gives Mr. Bisio a unique, feet-on-the-street point of view. His breadth of knowledge and experience as an entrepreneur allows him to approach business ownership from a holistic point of view.

As a public speaker, Mr. Bisio regularly gives presentations on the subject of franchising. He averages over thirty engagements a year. Mr. Bisio is often quoted by a number of different magazine and newspapers across the country.

When choosing advisors, it is important to know whom you are dealing with. Everyone claims to be an expert. Mr. Bisio is the real thing. In addition to the above-mentioned credentials, Mr. Bisio has also held Director and Vice President positions in franchising companies. During the 1990s, Mr. Bisio was instrumental in growing the brands Popeyes® Louisiana Kitchen, Church's Chicken, Seattle's Best Coffee, and Cinnabon® into over thirty countries.

Mr. Bisio earned his undergraduate business degree from the Simon School of Business at Washington University, St. Louis. He earned his Master in Business Administration and Master in International Management from the Thunderbird School of Global Management in Arizona.

BRITT SCHROETER

"Uniquely qualified." That is the phrase that best describes Mrs. Schroeter's appropriateness for working on this workbook. She has twenty-three-plus years experience as an entrepreneur, teacher, and franchise coach. She began her franchising career in educational franchising with Kiddie Academy Child Care Learning Centers, moving from Franchise Specialist to Executive Vice President during her tenure. Mrs. Schroeter broadened her exposure and expertise in franchising by working for Decorating Den Interiors®, Molly Maid®, Mr. Handyman®, and 1-800-DryClean®. From there, she became the Director of Franchise Development for Sylvan Learning Systems, Inc., propelling the system to the largest growth experienced in their twenty-plus-year history.

Growing up in a "restaurant family," Mrs. Schroeter saw the challenges of "going it alone." She also knows the value of a franchise first-hand, as she and her husband are franchisees for a premier service franchise. Ms. Schroeter not only "talks the talk" but she "walks the walk" every day, balancing her life between family, the family franchise, and her consulting practice.

For over a decade Ms. Schroeter has been an independent franchise consultant. She offers her extensive knowledge in franchising to individuals, partnerships and investment groups across the United States. With her guidance, a prospective franchisee can confidently make this key decision based upon her shared knowledge. Ms. Schroeter knows this workbook can broaden her reach, beyond the consulting practice to help others make smart business decisions. It is her goal that this book becomes a key resource from business classrooms in Cambridge to kitchen tables in Kansas.

In her spare time Ms. Schroeter promotes entrepreneurship as a guest expert for the International Franchise Association, *The Wall Street Journal*, *Inc. Magazine,* and on television, radio, and at speaking engagements throughout the country as a motivational speaker and content expert.

Ms. Schroeter holds a Bachelor of Education from the University of Maryland and a Masters in Business Management from The Johns Hopkins University. She lives in suburban Baltimore, Maryland, with her husband and two fun children.

CONTACT INFORMATION

If you wish to speak with Mr. Bisio or Ms. Schroeter directly, you can contact them at:

RBisio@educatedfranchisee.com

BSchroeter@educatedfranchisee.com

Include your name, email, and a little bit about yourself. They will then email you in order to schedule a time to speak.